Contents

Acknowledgements

To Gordon, my husband, who gave me time, space, inspiration, and guidance, throughout; and to all the wee ones for their hard work and helping hands. Also, to all those who have written to me, with advice, and encouragement over the years.

Preface

They used to laugh at, and deride the Victorian attitude that placed the Father in total authority over his wife, and his children also, until they were twenty one years old. They said it was barbaric.

They welcomed the emancipation of women and wives, and their equal responsibility for the welfare and happiness of their children.

Yet, by the 1970s they had happily embraced the notion, that the State itself could once again take on that authoritarian mantle, and dictate to children how they should behave, even while they were under 16; thus once again reducing the status and role of mothers, in such care.

Within the possible lifetime of a single woman, the wheel had turned full circle, against all mothers.

The 'they' to which I refer, are those indefatigable souls, sadly ever with us, who believe that they know absolutely best about everything – The Experts and Caring Professionals.

For three decades they had been conning parents, with Spockian follies and sociological fads; they had harangued and bamboozled parents into taking a back seat in family life. Pagan themselves or humanist, these experts sneered and jeered at Christian ethics, calling them 'primitive taboos'. They preached freedom-from-all-moral-restraint as the sure way to earthly paradise. These latter-day 'Lily the Pinks' – the Saviours of the Human Race – prophesied untold bliss in our liberated future.

But by the 1980s it was becoming increasingly clear to everyone that under such pagan philosophies, (which themselves relied so heavily on 'primitive taboos' to frighten us all into order) all was not as it had been promised. In fact, life was a good deal uglier, dirtier, more frightening and aggressive than before.

All the vices, which 'they' had said would disappear, were now at record levels, and were symptomatic of a thoroughly delinquent society.

It simply could not be allowed to get any worse.

Somewhere along the line, our ancient British Rule of Law must come to our aid, and protect us against those who seemed hellbent on manipulating social behaviour behind the scenes, in the classrooms and broadcasting studios, and including the arbitrary rule of Departmental Dictats within Government itself.

So much of the territory of parenthood had been encroached upon by 'interested' outsiders. Only a supreme act of revolt against this growing tyranny seemed to be the way forward. If we could not win back our freedoms by gentle persuasion or reasoned argument, then there was nothing for it but to 'go to law' and challenge this depressing degeneration in our midst through the highest courts in the land.

This book describes the progress of that long legal journey, over the single, simple issue of the right of parents to know about contraceptives being prescribed by doctors, to underage daughters.

Such a small request! Yet it called down upon its head the most furious antagonism imaginable; from the medical authorities and the DHSS, to the Agonised Aunties and every lunatic element on the fringes of socialist politics and birth control agencies.

But these people were way behind the times. They had almost become a part of the Establishment, itself, and its secular humanist philosophy. It was we, *the people*, who were now making all the running.

They tried to say it was all the work of something called the Moral Majority – or the Moral Minority – or the Moral Right – or the Moral Backlash. But what they *didn't* call it, because they daren't, was what it really and truly was: the Will of the People, declaring loud and clear 'enough is enough . . . .'

One: The Case Against
The DHSS – 1983

'Mother of ten, Mrs Victoria Gillick, wept in court yesterday, when a judge ruled she did not have the right to know if a doctor was putting her under-age daughters on the Pill. When he gave his decision in the High Court Mrs Gillick shouted, "God Almighty, that's ridiculous" and collapsed sobbing in her husband's arms.'

That was how the *Daily Express* reporter described the scene on that terrible Wednesday morning on the 27th July 1983. Yet, even then, I knew in my heart of hearts, that if the public were ever asked to vote on this one issue, 90% at least, would have given the thumbs down to the DHSS guidelines that had been causing all the devious and divisive problems for parents and their children. After all, I was asking for no more than common justice in family matters, was I?

I was the Plaintiff in the case; a mother of five daughters all below the age of 16, who lived within the area of the West Norfolk and Wisbech Health Authority, who brought proceedings to the High Court, seeking declarations from a Judge concerning a Health Service Notice issued by the DHSS in December 1980 (which itself, was a revised version of part of an earlier Notice, first issued in May 1974).

The section of that Notice on family planning (*sic*) for the under-age girl, was known to many people as the 'Notorious Section G'.

Because the 1980 guidelines were so closely linked to the previous 1974 ones, it is necessary, I think, to have a look at both of them.

The first version reads as follows:

'In 1972 there were 1,490 births and 2,804 induced abortions among resident girls aged under 16; these figures are vivid reminders of the need for contraceptive services to be available for, and accessible to, young people at risk of pregnancy, irrespective of age. It is for the doctor to decide whether to provide contraceptive advice and treatment, and the Department is advised that if he does so for a girl under the age of 16, he is not acting unlawfully provided he acts in good faith in protecting the girl against the potentially harmful effect of intercourse. The Department is also advised that other professional workers who refer, advise or persuade a girl under 16 years of age to go to a doctor in his surgery or at a clinic or elsewhere for the purpose of obtaining contraceptive advice and treatment would not, by such act alone, be acting unlawfully.

The Medical Defence Union have advised that the parents of a child, of whatever age, should not be contacted by any staff without his or her permission even though as a matter of clinical judgement the refusal of permission to involve the parents may affect the nature of the advice given to the child. Nevertheless, it would always be prudent to seek the patient's consent to tell the parents.'

Reading from the transcript of Mr Justice Woolf's declaration in 1983, he summarised my lawyer's objection to these guidelines, very clearly, when he wrote that we had submitted our case because we believed it:

'. . . amounts to the Department openly encouraging the provision of advice and contraceptives to girls under 16, with whom it is illegal to have sexual intercourse; that the advice suggests that it is for the doctor, and not for the parents of the child, to decide whether the girl under 16 should be provided with contraceptive advice and treatment, and that the doctor can be a doctor at a clinic who may not have any previous knowledge of the girl, so that he is wholly ill-equipped to deal with the socio-psychological problems

involved in   vide
contraceptive a   advice
on the law whic   at it wholly
disregards the leg   parents of the
girl in question . . .

These 1974 guidelines were drawn up by permanent officials at the DHSS, upon advice given them by the Family Planning Association and the abortion agency, the Brooks Advisory Services. The guidelines had drawn a lot of fire from individual parents like myself, and a wide range of family and church organisations, when they were first introduced, without any proper discussion of them in Parliament.

The heat was really turned on, in 1978, when the DHSS took its policy on birth control for school children, to its logical conclusion, and opened special clinics – (or Youth Advisory Services, as they were euphemistically called) for children. The newspapers got wind of them, and referred to them as they really were: 'Child Sex Clinics'.

Two years of solid opposition to the DHSS policy, brought about a promise by the newly elected Tory Government, that they would revise the wording of the guidelines, in accordance with their manifesto on the Family and Traditional Values etc., etc.

Medical journals reported the British Medical Association and others, as saying that, should the new DHSS guidelines be in any way *restrictive* or inhibit doctors from carrying on as they had been doing, for many years, then they would be automatically opposed by doctors.

Lobbying from both sides of the fence carried on apace, whilst everyone prepared for the coming DHSS revisions. When they were finally announced by the Minister for Health who was supposedly responsible for them, Dr Gerald Vaughan, the BMA *et al*, were delighted with them . . . and they passed by, unopposed in medical quarters.

Parents, on the other hand, were despondent beyond belief! For, to anyone with eyes to see, it had only been a

11

ques   fortable clichés,
surrou   on: that children
under 16 co   d the parents could
take a back sea   versus the true state
of affairs.

The actual wording of the revised 1980 version ran as
follows:

'There is widespread concern about counselling and
treatment for children under 16. Special care is needed
not to undermine parental responsibility and family
stability. The Department would therefore hope that in
any case where a doctor or other professionl worker is
approached by a person under the age of 16 for advice
in these matters, the doctor, or other professional, will
always seek to persuade the child to involve the parent
or guardian (or other person *in loco parentis*) at the
earliest stage of consultation, and will proceed from the
assumption that it would be most unusual to provide
advice about contraception without parental consent.

It is, however, widely accepted that consultations
between doctors and patients are confidential; and the
Department recognises the importance which doctors
and patients attach to this principle. It is a principle
which applies to the other professions concerned. To
abandon this principle for children under 16 might
cause some not to seek professional advice at all. They
could then be exposed to the immediate risks of
pregnancy and of sexually-transmitted disease, as well
as other long-term physical, psychological and
emotional consequences which are equally a threat to
stable family life. This would apply particularly to
young people whose parents are, for example,
unconcerned, entirely unresponsive, or grossly
disturbed. Some of these young people are away from
their parents and in the care of local authorities or
voluntary organisations standing *in loco parentis*.

The Department realises that in such exceptional
cases the nature of any counselling must be a matter for
the doctor or other professional worker concerned and
that the decision whether or not to prescribe

12

contraception must be for the clinical judgement of a doctor.'

As Judge Woolf recognised, these new guidelines, were an improvement on their predecessor; but noted our concern that they still encouraged the giving of contraceptive advice and treatment to under-age girls without consulting parents; and it still left the final decision as to whether or not to do so, to the clinical judgement of the doctor.

But how was it that I had managed to have these guidelines scrutinised in the High Court in the first place, some might ask? The answer is really quite simple.

When they appeared in 1980, amid great publicity, I felt that there was little more that I could do to put matters right, nationally; but I could and would ensure that my family, at least, would not fall foul of them. I had only four daughters at that time, and reckoned to having at least sixteen years ahead of me, before the youngest reached the age of consent.

With medical ethics seeming to rest, uniquely, in the hands of a few officials at BMA House and the DHSS, I thought it best to take steps to protect my daughters from manipulation by the profession, at any time in the foreseeable future.

So I wrote to our family doctor and to the local Area Health Authority in Norwich, and asked them politely, but firmly, for an assurance that none of my under-age daughters would ever be given contraception or abortion advice or treatment without *irrefutable* evidence of my consent.

Our GP came and visited us at once. He fully appreciated our worries, and accepted our point of view; being quick to tell us that he never gave such drugs as the Pill to a young girl anyway, as they were quite unsuitable – a man ahead of his time! So we were safe enough in that quarter.

But the Area Health Authority answer knocked me sideways! No – they couldn't give me any such assurances on behalf of their clinic doctors, as they were bound by the new DHSS guidelines; and *they* had said that confidentiality between a doctor and his patient was sacrosanct. Thus the final decision lay with the doctor, and his 'clinical judgement'.

I tried again and again to get them to abide by my forbiddance, in the interests of my children. All to no avail.

They even sent me copies of the new guidelines, as evidence that they were not just 'having me on', so to speak. From these I could see that a whopping-great loophole had been left for doctors, to simply carry on as they wished, irrespective of my known wishes or my legal responsibilities towards my children. Their interpretation of these guidelines was such that, where they had suggested that it would come into force only in cases where the parent was 'unconcerned, entirely unresponsive, or grossly disturbed', (and the child be given secret contraception), I was now being placed in this class of parent. It was a ridiculous Catch 22 situation. A doctor was free to prescribe, confidentially, if the parent was 'bad' – in order to protect the child and if the parent was 'good' – to protect the parent!

It was because of this, obviously contrived, piece of word-play in the guidelines (that might at some later date be employed against me) that I went to a lawyer and asked for his help. What were my legal obligations towards my children, in medical matters? Did I have the right to choose what medication was given them, or didn't I? Was the DHSS right, or was it wrong?

Well, two and a half years after that initial inquiry to a lawyer (and after innumerable tussles with the Law Society, who persistently refused to grant Legal Aid to assist our procedures on the grounds that our case was not in the public's interest, and did not have any public support!) we did eventually reach the High Court, assisted by Legal Aid.

The result, before Judge Woolf in 1983 is now a part of legal history – we lost the first round!

As the Judge scuttled out of the courtroom, leaving by a door behind his chair, utter confusion reigned. Lawyers, pressmen and friends all jostled together, whilst we stood, stunned. My husband, Gordon, standing beside me, ashen and almost in tears himself.

Perhaps he had had doubts all along, of our ever winning against such mighty bureaucratic odds. But I certainly didn't. Never for a moment, had I dreamed that such an absolute denial of my lawful rights as a parent, was possible. Was I naïve, or just blasé? At all events, it came as a most devastating blow.

I had been firmly convinced all along that nobody in their right mind would ever suggest that a doctor or surgeon could treat *any* child, whilst they were still the legal responsibility of somebody else, without gaining that 'somebody's' consent to act. Obviously there were exceptions to that rule, where a child had a sudden injury and no parent was immediately available. The doctor would be bound by commonsense, if not medical practice, to act as a good parent would want him to. He wasn't expected to bend down and whisper in the ear of a comatose child, 'Hold on a second – I've just got to go and get your mother's signature to this consent form . . . .'

Indeed, the whole question of parental consent to treatment in an emergency, had been made manifestly and dramatically clear to everyone, during the High Court case itself. On the very first day of the hearing, we were staying with friends at a house in Hackney, whilst our children were back in Wisbech, 'lodged' with various friends and relatives.

It was around 2 o'clock in the early hours of the morning, that we were both awakened by an unexpected telephone call. It was from King's Lynn General Hospital, who had 'phoned to say that our 10 year old daughter, Jessie, had been brought in to them, by the father of the family with whom she was staying, with suspected appendicitis. Could my husband come at once?

Yes he could! He threw on his clothes, and leapt into the car and roared up the motorway, breaking all speed limits on the deserted night roads, to be with her, in time.

While he was still on the road, an hour later, the hospital rang again. This time it was a woman doctor, who told me kindly, that they had decided to operate at once – and could they have my 'verbal' consent to do

15

so . . . . Naturally I gave it; then spent the rest of the night in a state of tearful suspense.

It was not until several hours later that Gordon himself 'phoned me to say that all had gone well and Jessie was now back in the wards, sleeping peacefully. He explained how he had arrived at the hospital to find staff quietly going about their night duties with the sick and emergency cases. They had been kind and helpful to him, as he sat by his daughter and held her hand as she was prepared for theatre. Then someone had handed him a consent form, which he duly signed . . . without comment . . . .

It is at such times that many parents appreciate all that is best in the medical profession; when doctors and nurses seem almost like heavenly beings – busy and efficient, but always with humour and gentleness.

It is at such times too, that one grieves that there are those on the fringes of this medical world, who seem almost incapable of appreciating the subtle and precious relationship between parents and their children, when the children are in trouble. If mothers or fathers become distressed and obstructive, even angry, at such times, it is just *because* that relationship is a total one; physical, emotional and spiritual. Their reactions are not unnatural, and they shouldn't be treated as such. Patience and kindness is all they need.

The news of Jessie's operation and the hospital's request for our consent to it, had reached the newspapers by the following day. I wondered hopefully, at this time, if the Judge himself had come to hear of it.

Later I learned that he had, and that he thought it must have been a Divine intervention! But it didn't sway his decision in the end. As he declared at the end of his twenty four page Judgement:

'. . . I find that there is nothing unlawful in the Department recognising, that in the exceptional case there remains a discretion for the clinical judgement of a doctor, as to whether or not to prescribe contraception.

This means, that as the Law stands at present, the

Plaintiff is not entitled to either of the declarations which she seeks. However, to put my decision in context, I would stress the following points: Firstly, if the Department's guidance is followed, it should only be in the exceptional cases that parents are not consulted. In the normal case of concerned parents, such as the Plaintiff, if the Department's guidance is followed, they will be consulted.

Secondly, as is indicated in this case, some Area Health Authorities are prepared to register with the local clinics, the view of parents.

Thirdly, even in the exceptional cases, the doctor, according to the guidance, has to exercise his residual discretion. In many matters concerning our health, we have to rely on doctors to act responsibly and, in this area, it is to be expected that doctors will exercise their responsibility – which is a heavy one – in a proper manner.'

Thus – 'in one fell swoop' – I found my children's moral safety was put at the most awful risk. We had so many years ahead of us; and there was nobody who could give me any feasible assurance, that one of them might not find herself caught up in this web of deception and folly.

The birth control agencies were naturally jubilant. Now, at last, they could carry on with their propaganda to the young that sexual expression was a human right, whatever your age, and whatever your foolish parents might think.

Outside the Court House, the Press milled around. From the outset, many of them had been encouraging and wished us luck. Now they looked glum, and some even angry. The questions they asked us, seemed to come from the heart; they were as upset as we were; so many of them being parents themselves, you see.

As they gradually drifted away, Gordon and I were left finally alone, to wander through the London streets and wend our way back home. How I cried and cried as the awful truth began to sink in: not only had I lost *my* rights as a parent, but the rights of all other parents besides. What had I done?

I dreaded the letters of recrimination, which I thought were bound to follow the judgement. Had I any right to place every other parent in so invidious a position? I should have left well alone, perhaps? But was it worse now than before; or was it now, simply, all out in the open? And was I wrong, anyway?

After all, my experience of fighting these perverse and ambiguous DHSS guidelines, for the past five years, had always shown that, when asked, the majority of ordinary people still believed they had a right to know about drugs of any sort being given to their children.

Between 1978 and 1980, had I not done everything democratically possible, to have the guidelines declared unlawful? Complaints to the Health Service Ombudsman; a petition of five and a half thousand names to Mrs Thatcher; speaking at meetings; writing to Ministers, MPs, Civil Servants, Doctors, Teachers and Medical Authorities. Letters in their hundreds had poured into Government, from people all over the country. Now it had come to its head, in an 'all out confrontation' as the papers say, and a single Judge had had to make the final decision about it all. What a task! Now that *was* a 'burden of responsibility'.

We returned to Wisbech, and during the following weeks were deluged with letters of commiseration. One of the first, from a lady in Littlehampton, helped greatly to summon our resolve to press on and not give up. She reminded us in her letter of the Ballad of Sir Andrew Barton:

'I am sore wounded but not yet slain;
I will lay me down to bleed a while
Then rise to fight again.'

Two: 'Before the Case . . . .'

> 'I appreciate that my decision will not only be
> extremely disturbing to the Plaintiff, but to many
> others who are naturally very concerned about the
> provision of contraceptive advice and treatment to
> those under 16.'

So said Lord Justice Woolf in the closing paragraphs of
his judgement against myself. How right he was: people
already were – *extremely* concerned!

The letters I had been receiving during the three weeks
that his decision lay in the balance, (and almost every
other letter which I have been sent since that time) by
parents, teachers, doctors, nurses and clergy, all
expressed the most profound distress and anger, at what
they had been witnessing or suffering, over many, many
years, as the erosion of happy family values and the
gradual corruption of the young gained unholy ground.

Yet all these letters, this 'crying in the wilderness' by
ordinary folk, remain almost totally unrecorded
anywhere. We pen an adamant letter, unburdening our
urgent message to somebody, somewhere, whom we hope
and pray might read it and take careful note; but knowing
in our hearts that within a few days – or even
minutes! – it will, as like as not, be crammed into a
waste-paper basket, or bottomless filing cabinet, to be
instantly forgotten.

Being but one letter, it cannot possibly have any real
effect, we say to ourselves. But we had to write it, had to
make the effort. Something we said, might just stick in
somebody's head, for a while, at least.

A few years ago, I used to send outraged letters to the
headquarters of the British Medical Association in
London, demanding immediate answers to controversial
questions, in no uncertain terms; and then becoming

increasingly impatient when the reply took longer than two weeks to arrive.

'That'll show 'em!' I used to think, as I defiantly tossed my little missives into the post box. Then one day I happened to find myself in Tavistock Square, outside BMA House. I couldn't see it at first, as I was expecting to find only a sizeable 'house'. In fact it seemed to take up half the street! Acres of building, several floors high. I stood in front of its vast gates, a mere dot on the landscape of medical bureaucracy. How in the world did I imagine that one little person could ever affect the thinking of this huge army of *quasi* civil servants?

Yet for some silly reason, I keep on writing to them!

But think of it another way: these private letters to public people, do actually form a consensus of opinion; and they are vitally important in any proper understanding of just what *is* the mood of the people, what it is they fear, their hopes, experiences and advice.

You may call it, as I do, 'the Will of the People'. Governments may try to override it, may even, on occasions seek to harness it. But they ignore it at their peril – especially at election time!

Newspaper and media editors are sometimes subtle enough to sense this mood, and even occasionally reflect it in their material. But for our purposes, and on the issue with which we are so concerned, they have not always been 'up front', as they say, in allowing that mood to express itself clearly. Instead, we have been almost stifled to death with articles and programmes crammed to the margins with the opinions of medical 'experts', Agony Aunts, women journalists, editors etc., etc; all apparently desperate to tell us how we *ought* to be thinking and reacting.

But what we want to know is what the average person actually thinks. We want to find out whether we really are the odd-ball reactionaries that some would have us believe. Are we really alone in our concerns; or are there others out there, feeling just like us?

Back in 1978 at a conference entitled 'Accepting Adolescent Sexuality', organised by the abortion agency charity, known colloquially as the 'Brooks', a well-known media man and educational psychologist, James Hemming, propounded his idea that since society had grown to accept that students in universities were likely to be sexually active, we were still denying that right to children in schools. That was the challenge, he said, that society had now to face.

Such liberalism, however, was not forthcoming to those who challenged views such as his in the first place. Well this little book attempts to give us some idea of what it is the public are saying about such things at the moment. It doesn't purport to answer all the questions, which would be an impossibility anyway, by anyone. But it does show that, not only do a great many people totally reject the Hemming vision of society, but that Governments themselves are wholly incapable of coping with the results of such a national capitulation to moral anarchy.

You may find, even with some surprise, if not a little relief, that those of you who are concerned about the current situation are actually not alone after all.

From the letters I received, it became clear that concern seemed to fall into certain categories, usually depending upon the motivation or occupation of the person writing. Thus they centred around suspicion of state control; worry over sex-education and the material used; worry about the physical effects of the contraceptive pill itself; the state of medical ethics and the seeming breakdown of family life.

One of the first letters I received, before the 1983 case was resolved, came all the way from a mother in South Australia. Even over there, the same phenomenon is being experienced, so it seems. The following is an extract of what she wrote:

Dear Mrs Gillick,

May I commend you on your stand against giving children the Pill without parents' knowledge.

I am constantly appalled at the high-handed way governments make moves to 'protect' our children. We have four daughters and it is a constant battle to guard them against outside influences until they are old enough to make responsible adult decisions.'

Another mother of six children, from London, put it in even more forceful terms:

'Thank God there are people like yourselves in our world, otherwise we would all be under the boot of bureaucracy.'

The feeling that, somehow or other, the 'Nanny-State-knows-best' dictum was all wrong, was expressed by a Devonshire mother who wrote:

'I only have three sons but of course they are also involved directly. I feel very strongly about the issue of parents' rights. Only too often the Authorities imply that we are amateurs and that they know best.'

Yet again a mother from Cambridgeshire gave vent to her frustration over the inconsistencies in the demands made by the state for parental responsibility:

'I felt I just had to write to express my absolute support for the principle for which you are fighting in the High Court; and indeed my admiration for your courage in 'taking on' the Establishment over this moral issue.

On the one hand we are told that parents do not take sufficient responsibility for their children's disciplinary training, and on the other hand we see this undermining of the parent-child relationship.'

The question of sex-education in schools: the people who teach it, and their value-free message to the young, has been a well-chewed bone of contention between many parents and teachers for years. A pharmaceutical chemist and Baptist Minister from Notts., put it quite simply thus:

We agree that much of the 'sex-education' given in

schools and by certain public bodies amounts to little more than encouragement of promiscuity and that it is having a serious and harmful effect on our national life. It is robbing young people of a happy and carefree youth.'

Of course, advocates of sex-education would say this was just a reiteration of inaccurate gossip, without any foundation in fact. They might also say that, far from spoiling children, it was enhancing their perception of their sexuality, and ridding children of a sexual neurosis inherited from a repressed older generation.

That may or may not be the case for some children. The point is, sex-education classes are *classes*, they are not individual consultations. So, for every child that benefits from such explicit references to their private lives or private parts, there is the child who reacts badly to it. I remember talking to a fourteen-year-old country girl, a few years ago, who had been crooning over one of my babies as I wheeled it out in the pram for the first time. As we talked, she told me how much she liked babies, but didn't think she would ever want to have any herself. 'Why on earth not?' I asked in some surprise. It transpired to be because she was terrified of the pain involved. Why did she think it was such an awful experience, that filled her with such dread? Then it all poured out: she and her classmates had had to watch a television film of the birth of a baby, during one sex-education lesson. It was horrible, she said, and had put her off the idea of ever having children at all. I tried to cheer her up, and give her the other side of things; but so much damage to her sensibilities had already been done, that I could only hope and pray that maturity and experience would undo the fear that such films had induced in her.

A school dental nurse from Devon wrote to me in more detail, giving her own experiences of some of the material published for children that she had come across:

'I think you would be very interested in some of the pamphlets issued by The Ministry to School Clinics and Health Centres on the subject of Sex Education for Teenagers, to quote one example:-

A leaflet on quarto sized paper with a two colour picture on the front depicting two young people deep in conversation, the girl's hands were on her knees, wearing no rings, with the caption overhead: *IF YOU DECIDE TO HAVE SEX WITH YOUR BOYFRIEND.* Inside it carried a very short paragraph on the various contraceptive devices, the sheath, intruterine devices, and the Pill and stated where and how these devices could be obtained. No facts were given regarding the failure rate of each of the various forms of contraceptives or the health risks with the Pill. The paragraph on Syphilis and Venereal Diseases was treated in a most cavalier fashion as something you might catch but that you could get treatment for. Once again no facts on the high risk of infection or the very serious consequences of these diseases to the teenagers or their children. Teenagers could be forgiven for concluding that these diseases were on a par with Measles or Flu! Finally, the question of the moral issue was not even mentioned on the pamphlet.'

Again, some might interrupt with 'What moral issues?' Surely contraception for the unmarried has effectively removed sex from the realms of morality? Is sex not just another aspect of that affection which any boy and girl might wish to share with one another? Modern sexual morality concerns itself not with the act itself, but with avoiding the pregnant consequences of it. Contraception has become a kind of social convention, rather like remembering to take a deodorant with you when you go to a disco party.

Against this kind of utilitarian thinking, parents have an uphill struggle. Twenty five angry parents wrote to me from Cambridgeshire with their own findings:

'We at this end are currently crusading over the method of teaching contraception to fifteen year olds in one local village college. We have found to our horror, that they are now viewing various contraceptives in class and have also graphic details given of how these are used. An hour or so is spent on this each year and an equal amount of time is given to the danger of sexually transmitted diseases. Somewhere along the line one must surely cancel the other out in value, not to mention the urgent need in our schools for the teaching of the old moralities and standards.'

But how in the world are modern teachers supposed to teach 'old moralities', when they themselves probably haven't a clue what they are! After all, many of them were teenagers themselves in the '60s; and it is that generation that first began to lose the way – or ignore it – as far as sexual morality is concerned. As like as not, many of them 'did their own thing'; so why should they try to stop others following suit? Perhaps we are asking too much of teachers to expect them to be moral as well as clever . . . . !

A former community education warden at a Hampshire school expressed the same disquiet at the content of this school literature when he wrote that he was:

' . . . appalled by some of the leaflets produced for young people by such organisations as Clocktower and the Brook Advisory Service, whose "advice" was solely at the practical level of how to avoid conception, and never at any time put forward a less superficial approach to relationships or included chastity before marriage as even worthy of consideration. I was certain, though I could not prove it, that the manufacturers of contraceptives had a hand in some of this literature.'

Controversial? Not really. It would be surprising if tobacco manufacturers didn't have something to do with cigarette adverts; so why should it be considered odd that Wyeth Pharmaceuticals financed the magazine of the National Association of Family Planning Doctors for some years; or that the contraceptive mail order company, FP Sales Ltd, should plough its profits back into the Family Planning Association and the 'Brooks'? Business is business after all.

On the receiving end of all this material are the children. Their mothers wrote to me about it. One of them, from the Isle of Wight, with a 12 year old daughter, was so worried about the idea that her child could be put on the Pill without her consent, that she had decided to go and tell her GP about her fears. She added that: 'Sad to say I would no doubt be treated as the neurotic mother!'

Actually, I don't believe she would be – at least I hope not. My own experience with our family doctor was extremely good. He came round at once, upon receiving my careful and politely worded letter, and gave my husband and me every assurance that he would never treat *any* child with contraception or abortion in a clandestine way. For him it was a matter of good clinical practice, apart from anything else.

From the point of view of 'good public relations' – or to put it another way, building trust between parents and doctors – it was an extremely wise move on his part. Perhaps some doctors don't fully realise just how important it is that this oft-quoted 'trust' be expressed out loud to parents. No good talking about it in general or abstract terms, in the medical press or elsewhere; people want to know how it applies to them in *their* case.

This Isle of Wight mother then went on to say something about the sex education in her daughter's school, as reported by the little girl, who, you will remember was only twelve, and just out of primary school:

> 'I also think sex education in schools is in need of a re-think, as my daughter tells me the talks they get on this subject never talk of love, marriage and respect for each other; how sad it is for our children and what great pressures at put on them by the methods by which they are taught. What can we do about it all? I feel so helpless and just hope and pray that my relationship with my daughter will withstand the strain that society is putting on us.'

Perhaps the child misunderstood the things said to her by the teacher? But that, surely, is what everybody is complaining about: children pick up different messages; consequently there can never realistically be what some hopeful souls call 'efficient sex-education'. A sex message is what you make of it, what you want it to mean – especially if you are young and curious!

A Lincolnshire mother with a 14 year old daughter took steps to keep such information strictly within the family. She wrote:

> 'I feel I must write and say how much I admire the stand you have taken against the medical profession.'
>
> 'I feel they have a lot to answer for in other areas too. Over use of tranquillisers etc., and it frightens me how they seem to have no moral sense. When I knew my daughter was to be given a contraceptive talk at school by the health visitor I kept her away from school. Like you I feel that is our department and not for the State to interfere in.'

I've done the same as she, myself in the past. You have to brave the critics though. The teacher who tells you that your child will be regarded as 'odd' by the others in class. Or that they will be 'out of step' with what the others are being taught. What, one wonders, will the 'others' be taught that I cannot impart to my own children, when I feel they are ready to need it? Perhaps they fear that I might not give them the full 'works', or might even – horror of horrors – not include contraception and abortion in my home instruction kit . . . . !

In any event, my children have never actually suffered one little bit, or been ostracised by their peer group. There are always plenty of other things to get on with in school, during the sex lesson. After the first week or so, nobody even noticed their absence from the class. One girl ever imparted to mine that she wished she could stay out of these classes too, as they were so boring!

A most perceptive letter came from a London mother of four, one of whom was a girl. She wrote early in July, before the Appeal result was known, about her daughter:

> 'Although she is not at a state school and will therefore

not be in danger of receiving the advice on contraception, I still feel that the effects of this sort of action by the DHSS reverberates through the whole of society and it becomes considered as an accepted thing for young girls to have sexual relationships with boys.

I feel there are probably many more people than we realise who would like to teach their daughters more about chastity than about contraception. There are probably many more girls who would like to know about chastity than we realise, but so little is spoken about such things these days.

Your point of course is the undermining of the fabric of the family and I think you are absolutely right, because once the family unit breaks up then the fabric of society as we know it also breaks up.'

Her last comments were soon echoed by a gentleman from an Evangelical Church in Suffolk:

'For too long these busybodies have been allowed to undermine the real structure of a nation's greatness, that is "Family Life".'

Over the last couple of years or so, the whole question of giving hormone steroids to adolescent girls to prevent pregnancy has come under close scrutiny amongst medical researchers. Papers have been written – and even disputed – about the harmful side effects of the Pill combined with promiscuity in young women. So much so, that ordinary lay folk have more and more come to understand some of the arguments themselves, and can argue the case with the best of doctors.

Some of them put it simply, as a grandmother from Birmingham did:

'It seems to me that doctors should not take it for granted that these children necessarily should have "sex" willy-nilly. They should tell the girls to say "no" and warn them of the physical and mental harm which free "sex" can do and advise them accordingly.'

Another lady from London was quite beside herself with

anger over the medical authorities' pronouncements on the Pill and young girls:

'Over the past few years, I have read with mounting horror and incredulity the amazing pronouncements of the BMA who seem to have gone power mad. In this case, not only are they usurping the parents' rôle, they are also acting with total irresponsibility from a medical point of view. Nobody knows what the effect will be on very young girls of this hormonal medication; permanent infertility may be one effect, and to whom will these girls be able to apply for redress then? Medical problems may also arise which will go undetected, or will be wrongly diagnosed, because neither the child's parents nor her GP knows of the medication she is taking.

If this madness is not breaking the law, then the law must be changed.'

A sixty five year old father of two grown up daughters, who declared himself to be 'not a Catholic', just to make quite clear that his was a purely medical concern, wanted to ask doctors two interesting questions:

'1. In the event of your daughter suffering side-effects or any other symptoms, would the doctor take your daughter into his own home for the correct cure?

2. Should your daughter misinterpret the Doctor's instructions and a baby comes along, would the Doctor take over the baby as his own, for he has taken over responsibility for the daughter's actions?'

A mother from Peterborough was just as angry with the BMA, General Medical Council and the DHSS; and gave her own experiences of how their combined policy was affecting the young:

'How on earth can we get through to those in authority? They are so *BLINKERED* they cannot see that lots of these children are and will need psychological treatment before they are grown up. They just cannot cope emotionally with premature sexual relationships.

As it stands at the moment I know of lots of very young girls (children), of course under 16, that are at their wits end over so called boyfriends who only go out with them for sex, which very soon loses its magic for the boys, and they are off with the next girl and the next, leaving the first girl out on a limb, suicidal, shattered and downright confused. Why can't the *POWERS THAT BE* see what is going on, and that the dishing out of pills is causing more confusion than anything.'

Two mothers of three young children, both from Bucks., just felt they had to write to me. They seemed to clarify so much of what is worrying parents today, about medical practice, the parents' rôle and child sex. The first wrote:

' . . . thank you for having the courage and the strength to take your stand on the *very* worrying question of doctors being able to take decisions affecting a child's whole physical and emotional and indeed moral future, without consulting with that child's parent or guardian, and it seems without even being that child's GP and without the benefit of seeing the parents' medical records – can this be even medically safe, let alone moral? Both my husband and I are extremely concerned about the whole matter, especially in view of the BMA's amazing ruling to actually try to prevent GPs from disclosing this information even when they would wish to do so. I take my rôle as a mother very seriously. I consider very carefully all the important milestones in their lives. We choose their schools, make decisions on vaccinations etc., and I am distressed and, yes, angry that there are people in this world trying to prevent parents from being involved in such an important question as their daughter being sexually involved while still under the "age of consent". For us all, parents and children, *KEEP UP THE FIGHT.*'

The second mother wrote that she was:

'. . . appalled at the way children are left in the lurch
by the very people who should be offering them care
and protection. We have a minimum age of consent
legally, and to offer contraceptive facilities to under age
youngsters without proper consultation with that
child's parents is negating the whole purpose of that
law. I firmly believe – and am supported in this by
my own teenage offspring – that there is no good
reason for the assumption that because a child is
biologically ready at 12 or 13 for full sexual
relationships, she is ready for the emotional side effects
of such action. There must be a time allowed for
innocence, in its old fashioned, pure sense, to be
allowed to blossom. The young people of today are
bombarded with advertising, media pontifications and
the like, all pushing them to adult ways before they are
ready or capable of coping. It is outrageous to take
away the parental right to guide a child in the ways of
truth, purity and respect – for herself and for others. I
am fortunate that when such situations have developed,
my daughters and step-daughter have felt enabled to
talk frankly and openly, and to seek my advice in the
first instance. I would deeply resent any attempt to
remove that closeness that we have, based on mutual
trust, by an outsider. For the sake of a horrendously
vulnerable generation, I pray that your action succeeds
and that these woolly minded individuals are stopped
once and for all in their attempts to wreck family life.'

There is only one point I would take issue with her, in that
splendid letter. For the most part girls are not 'offered'
contraceptives by a doctor; they *demand* them of him.
Abortions also. That is the doctors' dilemma; for many
doctors are no different to many parents: they capitulate
before this wilful onslaught. The question is – who
taught the children they had a right to 'demand' such
things of adults?

A publican's wife from North Yorkshire explained why
she supported the 'parents-right-to-know' position. She

also had some interesting observations to make about some parents:

> 'I do not want my daughters to be sexually experienced at fourteen or younger; they would lose their childhood and have nothing to look forward to. I want them to wait until they are much older and more mature. I will do my best as a mother but I don't want doctors going behind my back. It is criminal. We see a lot of what goes on with young people. I have to confess that most of the young people are very nice and sensible. I think it's the parents that I see who are more irresponsible and that is where the rot sets in. People should not have children if they are not prepared to see through all their duties from birth to adulthood. That includes loving and caring, and right from wrong, and all the manners, good and bad.'

Teachers too, see the problem at first hand; and those that are not 'sex-educators' themselves voice the same fears as others. One of them wrote to me from the Wirral, on a sheet of exercise paper, explaining 'forgive the paper – just a note scribbled in a hectic classroom. I am an English teacher in a very large comprehensive school'.

She went on to say that she was therefore:

> ' . . . well aware of the devastating effects of premature sexual experience on our young people. I have two daughters, of 15 and 11, and am both terrified and enraged by the possibility of them being offered contraceptive ''advice'' or appliances without my consent or knowledge.'

Another teacher from a state secondary school in London made two most important and salient points when she wrote:

> One aspect is *NEVER* discussed – the responsibility of parents to care for (i.e., feed, clothe, love) their offspring until at least the age of sixteen. If a girl is

turned out, technically the parents are liable, in court, for neglect. Another aspect, overlooked, is the effect on the education of girls whose main energies are channelled into premature unions, thus ensuring more half-educated young women, old before their time. It is, of course, the girls that suffer rather than the boys, by interference with the functions of healthy young bodies by hormonal pills. And whole generations of irresponsible young males are growing up without any feeling for the results of their activities – i.e., babies, who need years of care.'

It is certainly one of the oddest things, that so many amongst the Women's Liberation Movement have failed to understand this crucial point. That in every society that encourages, or condones, or expects its young females to be engaged in sexual relationships – whether inside marriage or out of it – the status and education of those girls falls behind that of the males. In our Western society, where this retrograde step is compounded by promiscuity, not only do the girls suffer through loss of educational and social advantage, but the males – as that teacher observed – grow ever more irresponsible, and yes – violent, towards the community in which they roam, uncontrolled.

A final letter to end this chapter comes from an Oxfordshire lady. Her letter touches on most of the points others have already made. But her concern as just another 'ordinary member of the public' is still worth noting:

'For the medical profession to connive seemingly at immorality in 15 year old and younger girls by issuing contraceptive pills, without even consulting parents, is horrendous. Do they also perform surgical operations without reference to parents? I am not sure about this, but "permissiveness" does seem to run riot. You are quite right to challenge the law to tidy up its attitude towards the young and the age of responsibility. Having sixteen as the age of consent, of leaving school, of criminal responsibility, the law should consistently uphold parental responsibility until that point.

As a teacher (now retired) I found it appalling that girls might be "taking the pill" on the understanding that they would indulge in sexual intercourse whenever opportunity offered. Parents must feel even more affronted.

Apart from the moral and legal issues, the Pill may have side effects, and not be compatible with other medicines, so the arrogant assumption that they can judge circumstances warranting it, positively makes my hair stand on end.'

Whenever I hear or read the loud protestations of the 'child experts' and sexologists, who seem to regard themselves as having almost mystical powers of perception and knowledge, I like to repeat to myself what this wise teacher wrote at the end of her letter:

'And how little do they seem to understand the young!'

Three: ' . . . And After It'

There are two vital elements which, more than any other, can galvanise a drooping spirit into action. The first is the knowledge that many people – a great many! – want you to go on fighting your corner; and the second is the prayers they promise you in that endeavour.

Somehow, you know that with such a potent energy at your back you are going to be carried along willy nilly!

So it turned out in our own case. We returned home to Wisbech, having failed to win the case before Judge Woolf, already full of determination to fight on. But we entered a house brimming with tearful children and long faces. The older ones were well aware of the issues at stake and were very upset by the outcome in London. They had listened to the result on the lunch-time radio news. The younger ones had picked up the atmosphere of distress, and were just as much in need of comfort and consolation. How cheered they all were when we made it quite clear to them at once, that it wasn't the end of the world! Just the beginning of a positive and lively campaign.

The very next day, messages began to pour through the letterbox. Not letters of recrimination as I had dreaded, but quite the reverse! A kind and inspired nurse from Huntingdon was one of the first to give us real comfort. She wrote:

'No doubt the disappointment was awful for both of you – but *do* take heart and start praising the Lord – because you've got the whole country talking and, I believe, alerted. This is, I believe, the beginning for many people. It's made me realise I've got to "get in" with both feet.

Don't forget that although the Lord's timing isn't always ours, it is always perfect! I just know that your

action was part of His plan, and He will bless you for
your steadfastness.'

A retired solicitor from Cheshire wrote something similar
and added further encouragement. Some journalists had
begun to wade into the fray with their oft-repeated
claim – not for the protection of the young – but for
the sexual rights of children. To this the solicitor replied:

'I beg of you be not disheartened by the fact that the
court decided against you and thereby to uphold the
pagan directive of the ministry. Was it Cardinal Henry
de Val (I think so, but I'm not quite sure) who said
something to the effect that in a godless society (which
is virtually the society in which we live today) the fact
that you are ploughing against the stream is strong
evidence that you are on the right course.

May you receive God's blessings a hundredfold on
what you have already done and on what you intend to
do.'

A Buckinghamshire lady from a national prayer group
gave us food for thought, with a quotation from Psalm 37
of the Good News Bible:

'Give yourself to the Lord, trust in Him and He will
help you.

He will make your righteousness shine like the
noonday sun.

Be patient and wait for the Lord to act, don't be
worried about those who prosper or those who succeed
in their evil plans. Don't give in to worry or anger, it
only leads to trouble.

Those who trust in the Lord will possess the land but
the wicked will be driven out.'

In each case we were being exhorted – quite
rightly – to *trust* in God, and not to despair. Like the
Baptist gentleman from Loughborough:

'You have my prayers and support for what you are
trying to do. Be encouraged by believing that with God

all things are possible. Bring everything to Him in prayer and be obedient to His directing.'

From Guildford, an Old Testament scholar and grandmother of 6, wrote with great feeling at the apparent duplicity of modern social policy:

'I know the great commandment "honour thy father and thy mother" can be translated into the plural, and honour given to all responsible parents, as there must be. Why all the fuss about Communist countries, forbidding parents to bring up their children in a Christian way, when we, who ought to know better, are doing this?

It would seem our country, for which many of us offered and gave our lives from 1939–1945, is becoming more lecherous and materialistic every day. The sexual experience is so much more important to women, seeing its consequences are so much greater.

We are *not* animals. To treat girls as sexual objects will bring the just wrath of God on those who do this. He will – as St Paul said – make them the victims of their lust, but they will drag others with them.'

From a Midlothian father came this widely held belief:

'I am becoming increasingly alarmed at the extent to which the legislation in this country is diverging from the Law of God. The Kingdom of Christ no longer reigns here and that is a terrifying state for any country to be in.'

The solace came in all shades and colours. Some more colourful than others! A Suffolk father of young teenage children wrote in the vein of Julius II, mixing mysticism with muscle . . . we well understood his feeling!

'Just heard the news on World at One. We send our best wishes. You must be pretty dispirited. Never mind, read Psalm 2. We'll find a way to hit the bastards!'

I had only to glance through the great pile of letters that were mounting up on my little desk, to know that people were outraged by the Court's decision.

Once again, the areas of concern were focused on certain key issues: the political and medical paradoxes; the rôle of parents and the harm to young girls.

A mother of seven grown-up daughters from Leicestershire reiterated the comparison between this government policy and the totalitarianism of some other nations:

> 'I am so glad you are taking on this nonsense about doctors giving girls the Pill without their mothers knowing. Isn't this takeover of parental rights by Rule of the State just exactly what people have been shrieking about in relation to the Communist states? This applies to those who have no religious view to fight for. They have picked on the tyranny of the State machine as being so heinous, and now are saying it is so beneficial for us in this exceptional case.'

A mother from Devon put it another way when she wrote that the Ruling of the High Court:

> ' . . . leaves me, and I'm sure millions of other mothers, speechless with horror. Are these judges trying to hasten the "Brave New World" that Huxley forecast?'

Sometimes the letters were short and to the point, as in this one from a lady from Shirehampton:

> 'I wonder if our children belong to us or the *State*.'

I don't know how many of these writers had read Lord Devlin's letter to *The Times*, published within a few days of the Judgement. Yet they were all saying essentially the same as he. You can well imagine how delighted and cheered we were to receive such support from so eminent a legal quarter!

'Social Importance of Pill Ruling
From Lord Devlin

Sir, The case of Gillick v West Norfolk Health Authority, on which you have just written an illuminating editorial (July 27) may well be socially the most important to come before the courts in this decade.

It is universally agreed that the upbringing of a child up to a certain age, in this case 16, must be subject to control. In the nature of things this must be either parental or State control. I think it to be the general belief that except in cases where parental control has clearly broken down, or where Parliament has clearly provided to the contrary, it is parental control.

This, although the law has not formally declared it as such, is a matter of public policy. At a time when courts of law were exceptionally timid someone arbitrarily said that the heads of public policy at common law must be taken to have been settled for ever somewhere about the turn of the century.

Lord Radcliffe, in my opinion the greatest lawyer of his generation, would not accept that. In a lecture on "The Law and its compass" he described the law on public policy as meaning "that there are some things the law will not stand for" and as "expressing those inner convictions that sustain the system itself".

He wrote: "We all feel that there are relationships arising out of human institutions which deserve special protection from outside invasion or even voluntary relinquishment" and he instanced first "marital and parental relationships".

I hope that in this case, if it goes further, or in one to come, the argument will not be restricted to speculation as to whether or not a crime may be committed or a trespass to the person. I hope also that the common law will be found still capable of giving an answer to the question of whether it is the parent or the health authority who is to decide whether or not a child under 16 is to be provided with the means of sexual promiscuity.

Yours etc.,
DEVLIN
West Wick House
Pewsey, Wiltshire.'

Old and young alike continually expressed their dismay at what they saw as another example of a nation going to pot! An elderly gentleman from Exmouth put it thus:

'Words fail me to express my disgust at that Judge's arrogance in presuming to tell you, and indeed all mothers, how to bring up their children morally, not in so many words, I know, but the implication was clear. I am now an OAP and so don't have the worry about the way children are allowed, and indeed encouraged, to act, although I do worry about the way the country has gone down morally.'

Whilst a young man from Putney in London saw it as a kind of self-inflicted problem:

'Like you, I find the decision of the Court extraordinary and very deeply disturbing in what it implies about the sort of society this country has created for itself.'

Many others were confused at the apparent perfidy of Tory Ministers at election times. This Londoner observed:

'Part of the present Government's Law and Order Manifesto was the declaration that they would "make parents responsible", and yet here is a glaring example of an extra-parliamentary body undermining the waning authority of parents.'

A music teacher from Hastings said much the same thing:

'I was astounded and shocked by the outcome of your recent court case, and further deeply disappointed by the lack of response by the Government (especially in view of Mrs Thatcher's public avowal of Christian principles), to help you in your inspiring defence of parents' (and indeed children's) essential Rights.'

One man from Cornwall thought we ought to take the whole case a great deal further at once:

'It seems to me that the Court's ruling goes against both the common law and the established Rights and traditions of family life that hold society together. I wonder if you are considering taking your case to the European Court. Some 16 months ago the Court ruled that caning a child at school in defiance of its parents' convictions about corporal punishment, constituted a breach of the European Convention on Human Rights. Surely the principles at stake in both cases are the same: The inalienable rights of parents to be consulted before a third party initiates action involving their children that goes against the convictions of the said parents.'

He may have been right in his advice about the European Court, but I have my doubts. For one thing, caning is a punishment for wrong doing and the Pill isn't. It was not so very long ago that a group of Danish parents went to this Euro Court to establish their right to withdraw their children from sex-education classes, which by all accounts were pretty horrid experiences. They lost their case. For some inexplicable reason, Western Europe is currently obsessed with the idea of contraceptive indoctrination of the young – and the younger the better – at almost any cost to the individual.

It seems to have something to do with a mad desire to reduce the birth rate in Europe to irreplaceable sub-zero levels. West Germany has the lowest population in the whole world, with only 1·4 children per woman. Never mind how sick, sad, weary and anxious we all are, in the process. Just so long as we are few enough to control, and old enough to tax!

A lovely long letter came from a couple in Bedford. It touched on a great many questions, and ended with a very appropriate quote from St Paul:

'The result of your courageous and conscientious efforts to stop an arbitrary and a dangerous circular, and to have DHSS directives to doctors concerning contraceptive advice etc., withdrawn, is sickening and very sad.

Parental wishes and authority are thus undermined,

even negated, while a doctor makes a far-reaching decision affecting the health, social practices, and family relationships of a young girl. A doctor who gives advice on contraception to a girl under sixteen, without the consent of her parents or guardians, acts in a grossly unethical manner. Yet, in a conspiracy of silence *with a child*, he is protected by Law!

The judge's comments were inept and unrealistic. *Of course* advice on contraception and the provision of "the Pill" encourages sexual relationships – smooths the way for a "first time" relationship and makes the continuation of established relationships much easier – a fact which many schoolboys, apart from older predatory individuals, know very well!

Above all, the very serious problems which your case in the High Court has brought to light, are moral and spiritual. There is an appalling moral landslide in our country and indeed, worldwide.

While a judge foolishly speaks of "the Pill" as a "palliative", those with more discernment know that he is expressing official policy and that one government department is under pressure from another, to reduce the *effects* of the landslide which they are unable to stop or control.

It is certainly true that "we do not wrestle against flesh and blood, but against principalities, against powers, against the rulers of darkness of this world, against spiritual wickedness in high places."

You will find peace, strength and joy even at this time, I trust, if you wholly trust the One who wholly loves you and died for you.'

St Paul's quotation was neatly summed up in a short letter from a mother in Weybridge:

'You've taken on powerful adversaries but you have right on your side!'

A Catholic solicitor from London made a point which, as a fellow believer, I read with a good deal of pain. I would that he was wrong. He ended in hopeful vein though, and with an astute observation about society:

I am of the same opinion as you and many right-thinking people, in that parents, not the State or the medical profession nor anyone else should be arbiters of our children's health or morals. The right of parents must be permanent.'

Well, what do you think of that? Would boys treat girls in a more civilised and respectful manner if they could be persuaded to regard all women as precious from their babyhood upwards – or by reminding them to use a condom while they had sex with girls? As for some of her other questions, the answers may be found elsewhere in this book, from the mothers of girls put on the Pill behind their backs. They make sorry reading.

Another mother from London related the views of her cousin, and then added her own thoughts:

'My cousin is a District Nurse. She told me "If these women only knew what their wombs looked like after the Pill, they wouldn't take it!" Also indirectly the Pill opens the door to sexual freedom at an age when the *PARENTS* are still legally responsible for her breakdowns, broken love affairs etc. In other words *we* are still responsible for the *mess* the DHSS are causing. The side effects of the Pill are still not completely known, but I can tell you no happiness is found by a girl feeling tempted and free to do as she wishes. A boy *obviously* takes advantage of this. To conclude, cancer and herpes are known to be caused through early, frequent sex, so this is another point. All the while a girl says "yes" a man will never marry. Sex is for the comfort and intimacy of two people committed to each other in marriage, ideally. The blessing of their union is a child. No one should indulge a man's greed.'

From a well-travelled Surrey man came these points:

'Society has to reverse the trend that sexual intercourse practiced on the scale it is today, and by the young and immature, is not the normal way of life and if persisted in, virtually precludes a happy and successful marriage

45

in later life. The high divorce rate of 1 in 3 must be related. There is also the serious risk of sexually transmitted disease and not least AIDS, for which, it seems, there is no known cure. The medical profession is bucking the issue by hiding behind the confidentiality of medical treatment.

I find it very sad when I travel abroad to hear this country mentioned as being sexually promiscuous as well as having the second highest divorce rate for a civilised country.'

A Methodist mother from Plymouth took up the medical questioning again in relation to clinics:

'What of the girl's medical history? A young girl cannot be expected to remember information which might preclude her from being put on the Pill – except at unacceptable risk. What about the mothers who took Stilboestrol during their pregnancies? Their daughters are already at great risk of cancer of the vagina; the Pill would greatly aggravate that risk.

If these clinics truly want to help the girls, and not just sell pills, via the NHS, why don't they make it a rule that the man or boy in question comes along with the girl? Many, many boys would be too ''embarrassed'' to face up to the situation in this way. If the boy refused, then the girl would be able to defend herself from his pressure to have sex with him; it would be *his* fault, *his* responsibility. She would see him in his true light, a greedy little boy, ready to snatch at any pleasure, but not ready to face up to any reality.

How do clinics know that the girl has a steady relationship and is not just sleeping around, unless she can persuade the boy to present himself?

As to the legal aspects, words fail me. It seems that now our doctors can change the laws of the land without any recourse to Parliament or the statute book. What sort of a lousy country *are* we living in?'

The lady obviously hasn't realised yet that clinic doctors are more likely to give the Pill in secret to a girl who *is* sleeping around, than to one who isn't. Indeed, the more bizarre and hazardous the sexual liaisons, the more the Pill is prescribed. For example, incest is *prima facie* evidence of the need for contraception, by the abused girl, according to the Family Planning Association.

Is there any truth in the suggestion put forward by the next lady, from Essex?

'I think that those doctors would not be so ready to take charge of the welfare of the children if they had to find the money from the parents, instead of getting it from Government's dispensing of taxpayers' money, and from companies who promote their products at the youngsters' expense. Is it still the law that a child cannot be held financially responsible for goods ordered and that the seller has no redress if the parents won't pay? How different the Government's attitude is here, if that's the case.

What is to stop clinics advising boys to have treatment, operations or drugs, that would increase ability to win at sport? This is becoming more and more the acme of attainment. Yes, I know, "It can't happen here". I wonder!'

Well, actually BUPA insist on a parent's consent to their children's treatment, right up to the age of *eighteen*, the age of majority. The lady was accurate all right!

Naturally enough, there are those people who believe, honestly, that this whole debate has done nothing more than frighten a great many more girls out of the doctor's waiting rooms, and almost inevitably into pregnancy, due to lack of contraceptives. Then again there are those who dishonestly promote this idea, as a way of scaremongering amongst a confused and worried public. I say 'dishonestly', because by and large the most vociferous groups lobbying in this way, are those who have all the facts before them, and who are well aware that from Government statistics, the conception rate amongst the under 16s has been steadily rising again, since 1980 – five years ago! So I cannot be blamed for that upward trend, can I?

Now, before anyone says: 'Ah yes, but you are fudging the figures to suit your own case', let me say at once that I am only quoting Government statistics, as reported by one of my most ardent adversaries, the 'National Abortion Campaign'. Let me quote them in full:

'The conception rate for under 16s rose between 1969 and 1972 (as did the conception rate for all women) when it reached a peak of 9·2 conceptions per 1000 women aged 13 to 15. The conception rate fell to 7·1 in 1980. In 1969 only a quarter of under 16s who became pregnant had an abortion. However after rising slightly between 1969 and 1971 the maternity rate for under 16s fell from 5·5 to 3·9 in 1975. During this time the abortion rate more than doubled so that since 1975 most under 16s who became pregnant had their pregnancies terminated, although the conception rate fell between 1972 and 1980. Recently it appears to have started rising again with corresponding increases in the abortion and maternity rates.'

Newsletter NAC April–June 1985:

What kind of numbers are we talking about? Well, according to this organisation's Government figures, there were 543 abortions on girls under 16 in 1968, and 4,087 in 1983 – the highest ever. The number of overall conceptions, resulting in birth or abortion, in this age group rose from around six and a half thousand in 1969 to eight and a half thousand in 1981 and is rising steadily each year since.

Government figures also show that 1980 saw the greatest number of pregnancies since 1969, to eleven and twelve year old girls (perhaps I should have said 'under-age women') with 17 of them giving birth to babies, and 22 having them aborted.

Once again, according to the National Abortion Campaign, 'Women under 16 are more likely to have a late abortion than older women . . . about 7% of women having very late abortions (i.e. over 20 weeks gestation) are under 16.'

48

Sexual liberation has done wonders for our primary and secondary school children . . . .

So if, in the next year or so, you hear the cry go up 'The awful Gillick-ruling has caused more girls (under-age women) to become pregnant!', please bear these facts in mind. They were *already* rising, before ever Gillick came on the legal scene. They will continue to rise, inevitably and inexorably, if the number of girls trying to use the Pill properly – and failing – continues to increase by tens of thousands each year as at present.

On the other hand, if the number of girls going on the Pill should suddenly drop by half, over the next year or so, and the pregnancy figures *don't* double-up correspondingly, then it might be because parents like this one from Co. Durham are taking steps to ensure that they talk to their daughters first, before others outside the family can get an unhealthy look in:

'I have five daughters, the eldest being fifteen, and I wasn't fully aware of this contraceptive dilemma until you brought it to the attention of the media, and for that I wish to thank you.'

Again, from Northumberland a mother writes of her change of heart:

'When you first hit the headlines, I don't think I really agreed with your campaign, as I was all for the right to privacy in matters of an adult nature. I am sure we both know not even married women get that. Now I have had time to re-think the situation I wish to offer my support. Obviously by withholding the information in question from parents, the medical profession are withholding the names of those with whom these children are having associations, and I believe that to be your aim behind your effort. Children have to be protected from themselves as well as from others, and we know full well that we cannot point the finger of suspicion in any one quarter until we have all the facts.'

Many parents have resented the fact that these DHSS guidelines to doctors are a 'catch-all' policy, hurting good and bad families alike.

That was inevitable I suppose, despite DHSS protestations that they were only meant for 'exceptional cases'. What is all right for one girl becomes all right for any girl. The notion of 'parents-keep-out' is an indiscriminate one, in the long run. And it has been an awfully 'long run' . . . .

A woman teacher from Scunthorpe saw its pitfalls thus:

'Parents' rights are being eaten away and the "State" is becoming all too powerful. When we bring children into the world as responsible parents, we are prepared to bring them up in the true Christian way. What right has anyone or anybody to say what is good for our offspring?

For a child to be given contraceptive drugs and devices, secretly by a doctor, is teaching the child to be deceptive and destroys the parent-child relationship. It makes me see red.'

One might also add to that, that teaching a child to be deceitful destroys *all* trusting relationships with that child, by anyone. It is a habit, once learned and practiced successfully (with the aid of another 'respected' adult), that becomes very hard to lose, as time goes by.

A major concern of many people, as has already been seen, is the way in which the 1983 High Court ruling seemed to ride roughshod over commonly held ideas about parenthood. Eight law students from five different universities wrote together of their 'dismay' at this aspect of the case:

'We have been following your High Court case with great interest over the last weeks. We are extremely grateful to you for your courage and determination in pursuing this course so far. We heard the judgement of Mr Justice Woolf last night with dismay, and we have read various reports and editorials of the serious press this morning with horror.

It is obvious that Judge Woolf has brought about a major miscarriage of justice and, in setting a precedent in Common Law to the effect that parents have no rights concerning their children's sexuality, has dealt another dangerous blow to family unity. We would like to urge you, most strongly, to take this case further, to the Court of Appeal, so that Mr Justice Woolf's judgement might, hopefully, be overturned.'

It was also the harm being done to young girls which made many people so outraged. A parent/governor of a Hampshire school explained her own concern:

"FPA clinics in this area are not able to counsel young people properly, and have to cope with very young girls turning up without parents, let alone their knowledge of what they are doing. I am concerned about sex "teaching" in schools – the young people are, I am sure, falling through gaps of not knowing what they are assumed to know and without ethical instruction.'

Another parent from Eastbourne saw the problem on a wider scale:

'There is no need to draw your attention in detail to the heart-rending cases of child abuse and disgraceful practices that are now being *un*covered daily which must shock the nation into *demanding* government intervention. These all attained *far* more publicity than normal because of your own initial challenge on the matter of deprivation, which touches the conscience of every parent: "where the cap fits"!'

Well now, you can read that both ways I suppose. For if children are being abused *by* their parents, the argument for parents falls down to some extent, doesn't it? Or so the DHSS would say. But I would add, that in those cases where children are being abused within the family, that family needs help. The child will fare no better if supplied with a headguard or metal vest as a palliative against the consequence of a crime against them. No more would contraceptives protect them properly against incestuous sexual abuse. Bad parents need careful sifting from the good. There aren't that many of them, so bad that nothing can be done to help. To lump us all together is a downright injustice.

51

A mother (no address given) wrote to me via the BBC. Her feelings are shared by many, many others. What she says about the young men is conveniently overlooked by those who promised 'girls' liberation':

'What you have done will not only help your under-age children, but many thousands of little girls who are having their lives ruined by the sexual lust of boys and men. Love does not come into it, but only lust. The lust of deflowering under-age girls, with a lifetime of tragedy following in its wake for the girls, even if they don't become pregnant or diseased. A child under 16 does not know what kind of person she wishes to be, and to have sexual intercourse thrust upon her when she is only a child is terrible. These boys and men only despise and talk about her afterwards, adding insult to injury, and therefore also ruining her reputation as well.

Parents and girls will be most grateful to you for combatting the State's intrusion into family life. Instead of the State giving an underage girl the Pill, they should be reporting the boy to the Police as he's breaking the laws of the land by having unlawful sexual relations with an under-age person. But the State allows these men and boys to get away with it. It's time they were brought to book.'

A Hampshire lady even suggested that the Equal Opportunities and Race Discrimination Laws might be invoked, because of the unfair way girls were being treated:

'The *spirit* of both these laws could surely be applied to your case against the prescribing of the contraceptive pill to young girls, because:-

(1) Such girls are being denied equality of opportunity to grow up free from the possible hazards of long-term consumption of drugs;

(2) Such girls are being discriminated against, in that it

is they, not the boys, who are required to consume the contraceptive pills.

It could be said that these girls are being treated unequally, and are being discriminated against, for the sake of convenience now. In later life they could be distressed and angry that they were given a powerful drug over a long time-span and they could seek compensation for failure to protect their long term wellbeing.'

The commercial pressures upon the public in general are huge; that we all know. They come to bear upon the young with even greater force. So too, the need to conform with the tribe – the peer groups. Keeping up with the mini-Jones's, as you might say. A Birmingham mother gave her views on this point:

'There is a great deal of pressure on teenagers to indulge in early sexual experimentation. This was certainly the case when I was at school and as I have now reached the ripe old age of 31, I can only assume that the pressures are even greater now.
    Now that it is public knowledge that contraceptives can be supplied without parental consent, a great many more young girls will certainly succumb, albeit unwillingly in most cases, to these pressures. I think this situation is scandalous and I sincerely hope that your case will be successful in the Court of Appeal.'

A teacher from Lincolnshire saw it all, as it will inevitably be seen in years to come. It is a sad comment indeed:

'As a Quaker to a Catholic, may I just say how much I applaud the stand you have taken. My own three children are now grown up, but I am still teaching teenage girls after many years, and it grieves me to see how their purity is constantly assailed by a decadent society which seems hell-bent on destroying the next generation. Thank you for having the courage to stand up for what you know instinctively to be right. God Bless.'

Four: 'The Public Petition'

'Please do not give up the *FIGHT*' wrote a mother from Surrey on the 27th July 1983.

I certainly didn't intend to. Not after so many letters had come thudding in batches on to my doormat!

However, as the early August days passed by, it was difficult to see just what I *could* do. Our lawyers had already declared their intention to appeal against the High Court decision; but somehow I felt that even more had to be done before then – and quickly – since rumour and speculation had put the date of the Appeal before Christmas 1983.

By hook or by crook, the Government had to be made to wake up to the fact, that the entrenched position of the Health Department was extremely unpopular with rather a large number of people. But how to do it?

As has so often happened during these last couple of years, a particular letter, from a previously unknown individual, has 'charged my batteries', so to speak, and given a further impetus to this campaign for true social justice.

Such a one came from a father from Essex the day after we lost the case in the July. I call him a 'philosopher-poet', because his letter had that quality about it of a wider vision of society. The utilitarian arguments of Governments in office, and medics in practice, can scarcely serve to help us see the whole nature of our modern dilemma, as it must be seen. True poets and true philosophers do not merely reflect society, casting back its own image upon itself. They reflect *upon* society; its historical developments, its spiritual journey. This is what he wrote:

'I am most disappointed that your attempt to re-establish a degree of legal morality into medical ethics

54

has failed. It is indeed a sad reflection of our society that the state of the Law is directed by popular demand rather than the protection of the innocent.

Some thirty years ago, as a young constable, I stood outside the Central Criminal Court and read the inscription above the door ''Protect the children of the poor and punish the evildoer''. For years this and other tenets stood as my yardstick in the practice of my office. Sir Thomas Moore, our most perfect model Lord Chancellor and Judge, once said ''If Law were to become the instrument of fashion, God forbid, then lawyers should pack up their books and go home; then none of us will sleep easy in our beds.'' This more than any other, echoes in the unjust sounds we have heard in the so called ''Family Division'' of the High Court.'

So many people were upset at what had happened; so many voices crying out to be heard. What was I to do? How could I harness them all together and give *them* the opportunity to be heard above the din of media pontifications? Suddenly the answer came – a Public Petition. Of course! It was obvious once I had thought about it. Let the people speak for themselves. A properly written, carefully worded Parliamentary Petition. Not the usual sort; but one that I had heard about, and even used myself on another issue, only the year before. It was an ancient 17th century method, of allowing the people of a constituency to use their Member of Parliament as a kind of Herald, to the House of Commons, on their behalf. The MP didn't even have to agree with the petition necessarily. But provided it was not seditious or entirely stupid, and was properly written out by hand using the precise, if antiquated, wording of those bygone days, then only the ignorant, ill-mannered or utterly intolerant would refuse to present it on behalf of their constituents.

This Petition would be a genuine *vox populi*. Thousands and thousands of people all calling for a change to that invidious DHSS Ruling . . . . That would make the Ministry sit up and take note, if nothing else would!

Initially, the wording of it was the biggest hurdle to overcome. For days I chewed over various ideas for it, tearing off my rubber gloves in the middle of washing up to scribble them down on the backs of envelopes, muttering away to myself as I scrubbed the kitchen floor. Plenty of good ideas came, but somehow I couldn't find a clear line of thought, couldn't find the right beginning. It had to say so much, yet at the same time had to make immediate sense to anyone who read it.

Then out of the blue, a marvellous mother from Cardiff dropped me a line – in more senses than one – with the words from the Universal Declaration of Human Rights.1242

That did it! I had the basis for the Petition. The Universal Declaration stated that the family was entitled to 'special protection' by society and the state. Well, at the present time in Great Britain the family was certainly *not* getting that. The rest of the wording came pretty quickly. Then it was printed by a local firm in Wisbech and paid for out of all the donations from the public that had poured into the 'fighting fund'. Next, they were sent out to anyone and everyone who wrote and asked me for a copy. Six thousand in all; and countless more photocopied afterwards, by others. The Petition was 'on the road'. It was unstoppable now!

Here is what it said:

Public Petition

To the Honourable the Commons of the United Kingdom of Great Britain and Northern Ireland in Parliament assembled.

The Humble Petition of the Residents of the Constituency of . . . Sheweth that we the Undersigned oppose the 1980 DHSS Revised Health Service Notice (Section G) which advises doctors that they may provide contraceptive drugs or devices to girls under the Age of Consent without their parents being consulted. We oppose it for the following reasons:

1. In 1885 the Age of Consent was fixed by Statute Law at 16 years. This made it unlawful for any male to have sexual intercourse with a girl under 16. This was

expressly to protect those young girls who were considered at risk from immature sexual relationships. Girls from poor, uneducated or deprived families were considered to need even more protection than those from more stable homes.

2. In 1983 young girls are just as vulnerable to the hazards associated with early sexual relationships; including modern medical and sociological evidence of cervical cancer, sexually transmitted diseases, pregnancy, abortion, promiscuity, depression, suicide and prostitution.

3. Modern medical research has also pointed out that powerful hormone contraceptive drugs (oral and injectable) and internal devices carry with them substantial risk both in the immediate and long-term health of immature females, by affecting detrimentally the healthy, developing pituitaries and ovaries, and can cause, amongst other things, cancer of the cervix and breast, pelvic inflammatory diseases, retardation of bone growth, deep vein thrombosis, aggression and sterility.

4. Children make very poor candidates for the regular, daily self administration of contraceptives. The contraceptive failure rate amongst teenagers is extremely high. Hence the following statement by Dr Judith Bury of the Edinburgh Brooks Advisory Centre in June 1981: 'There is overwhelming evidence that, contrary to what you might expect, the availability of contraceptives leads to an increase in the abortion rate.'

5. Girls need special protection, as the future mothers of society, and must be given opportunities and facilities, by law and by other means to enable them to develop physically, mentally, morally, spiritually and socially in a healthy and normal manner.

Wherefore your Petitioners pray that the Honourable Members of the House of Commons should bear in mind, that according to Article 16 of the Universal Declaration of Human Rights 'The family is the natural and fundamental group unit of society and is entitled to protection by Society and the State.' We ask that they should therefore urge the Home Secretary that he should recommend to the House that Parents must be given *STATUTORY RIGHTS* to be *CONSULTED* before any contraceptive drugs or devices be given to their daughters whilst they are under 16; thus enabling parents to take whatever action they think necessary to protect their daughters from early and unlawful sexual relationships, and the criminal actions of the males involved.

And your Petitioners, as in duty bound, will ever pray . . . etc.

Every evening from August onwards my little sitting room table wobbled under the growing pile of letters, petitions and envelopes. I sat addressing, licking, sticking and stamping them way into the night, tottering wearily but cheerily off to the Post Office with a bulging bag of them every morning. The fight was on – in earnest!

As soon as I was ready, I let the Press know all about it. It was essential that as many people as possible came to hear about it and wrote to me for copies.

I hoped that, by October when Parliament re-assembled after the long summer holidays, these parliamentary missives would be ready for presentation. MPs had been warned by their constituents to expect them. Actually, some of the MPs were so unaware of this ancient procedure that it took a while to educate them in these old-fashioned democratic ways!

An MP would be sent a Petition by post; he would then take it into the House of Commons on a Friday morning, and, with the Speaker's permission, would stand up and read the top copy out loud; then he would bow to Mr Speaker and walk solemnly round behind his Chair and place the Petitions in the green Petition Bag. Whichever Minister they were directed to would eventually receive them on his desk.

Those MPs who were unable to read them out would simply place the Petition in the Bag, at any time during the week.

If all went as planned, the proceedings of the House would be halted for several minutes each Friday morning for several weeks, thus ensuring that the message contained in the Petition was well and truly hammered home!

Some Members who actively supported the Petition said that such a strategy was misguided and wouldn't work. Better to have all the Petitions presented in one batch, they said, as was 'normal'. But that was the whole point behind the plan – it *wasn't* normal! Thereby it would draw greater attention to itself. MPs might not like it at first; but they would soon see how effective it was. If democracy was going to work at all, it had to be seen *AT* work. MPs are our elected representatives after all. Then let them represent us, when our need is greatest.

However, the publicity for it got off to a rather bizarre start, as a result of the Press not quite fully understanding how the Petition was being organised. They reported, accurately enough, that I had made a request to my own MP, Clement Freud, to present the Petition from his own constituents to Parliament, later in the year. Then a Harley Street consultant orthopaedic surgeon wrote a splended letter to the *Daily Telegraph* criticising the General Medical Council on its own policy on contraception for the under 16s. Unfortunately he also mentioned that Freud was presenting a Petition to the House of Commons on my behalf, and invited readers to join in and write to Freud giving him their support. As this doctor's letter was so extremely important, I include it here:

The Daily Telegraph – Saturday August 20, 1983

Law On The Pill Needs Changing

Sir – You quote (report, Aug. 18) from a General Medical Council document about consent for prescribing the contraceptive pill for girls under 16.

This simply states the position as we have known it

for many years, but of course that does not make it any more palatable to those of us (parents and doctors) who think the law needs to be changed.

What is not perhaps appreciated by parents and even some doctors is that the law permits doctors to give treatment including surgery to children under the age of 16 without there being any statutory obligation on the part of the doctor to obtain consent from the parents.

Furthermore, there is no obligation to inform the parents, either before or after the event, if the child says that it is not their wish.

Clearly it has always been the practice of the majority of clinicians to obtain consent from parents for investigation and therapeutic measures, especially operations. In an emergency, a doctor may have to proceed without consent or simply with verbal consent; in some circumstances he will take on the responsibility himself if delay in obtaining consent would be likely to prejudice the child. All this is commonsense practice and is supported by the Medical Defence Union and the General Medical Council.

The recent High Court action brought by Mrs Victoria Gillick highlighted the problem. In particular Mr Justice Woolf made it clear in his judgement that consent in these cases is not obligatory for any medical procedure including prescribing the contraceptive pill.

It is my opinion that there is an urgent need for a change in the law with regard to consent for medical examination and treatment of children under 16, and I include contraception under this heading.

I wish to see the law changed so that it is obligatory at the very least to inform parents that their child is in need of medical treatment, and also in those cases where investigation and treatment has been instituted without parental consent, that it would still be obligatory to inform the parents of what has taken place.

These are minimal changes but preferably in non-emergency cases I hope it would become obligatory to obtain consent before examination, investigation and treatment starts.

The present fashion of allowing sexual freedom for children under 16 has disguised the fact that all medical treatment is governed by a similar emotional attitude of those so-called liberal-minded folk who want total freedom for children to choose for themselves without any guidance from their parents. The law must never be subject to such changes in fashion for this is the road to moral degeneration.

I think there is a silent majority of parents and doctors who would like to see a change in the law along the lines I have proposed. I hope they will be less silent and write to their MPs and the General Medical Council or write to Mr Clement Freud, MP, who is presenting a petition to the House of Commons on behalf of Mrs Gillick.

Unless they do, the present increase in loss of distinction between a child and an adult will continue, and there can be no prospect of producing a necessary raising of moral standards of future generations.

I think this matter is important, but I appreciate that there are a minority who do not take the same view; unfortunately they have had the loudest voice of all.

Nigel H Harris
Consultant Orthopaedic Surgeon
London W1.

Not surprisingly this 'call to action' brought scores and scores of letters all pouring into Mr Freud's office. I know this for a fact — because he kindly sent them all on to me!

Unfortunately – or I should say ironically – dear Clement didn't actually support the Parents' Campaign at all. Not one little bit. Nor had he done so, right from the beginning. His liberalism seemed to have stopped short, somewhere back in Victorian England, *pre* the great social reforms!

But I had written to him nonetheless, requesting that he be the one to present the first Petition in October. However, he let me know quite bluntly, that if he were to do so, he would feel morally obliged to speak *against* it. Moreover, from his long parliamentary experience, he said, he did not believe Mr Speaker would tolerate more than one Petition to be read out on any one issue. Added to that, he was *never* in the House on Fridays anyway (he said!). Hastily I made arrangements for Sir Bernard Braine to present my constituency petition along with his own. A merciful provision for those poor, benighted souls left stranded with a disobliging Member.

It was therefore rather amusing that so many people wrote to Mr Freud to congratulate him on his brave stand! I do hope he read all these letters, before passing them on to me; they were so good; and without doubt, an unprejudiced mind would have learned a great deal from them in the process.

Amongst those who wrote to him, it was the members of the medical profession who, most vociferously and roundly, condemned Mr Justice Woolf's judgement. A Consultant Neurologist wrote:

'Dear Mr Freud,
It seems incredible that the Law should deprive parents of the control of their own families, and that the medical profession should facilitate promiscuity, with all its attendant medical and social hazards, in this furtive way. We would therefore like to thank you for raising the matter, and to lend our support and best wishes to your petition.'

While a Nottingham GP and his wife reiterated once again, probably as parents as well, the responsibility angle:

'May we request that you do all in your power to reverse the unwise judgement that under age persons can be put on the Pill without the consent of the parents. In an age when all teenage ills are said to be due to the lack of parental control, then to further undermine this control will bring its own dire consequences.
We are moving into an amoral society due largely to the efforts of a very vociferous minority. May we thank you for your wisdom and concern in taking up this worthy cause.'

Two Psychologists from Essex pointed out the confusion over the oft-quoted 'clinical judgement' of a doctor:

'In our view there is an urgent need for a change in the law with regard to consent for medical examination and treatment of children under the age of sixteen, which should include the prescription of contraceptives. We are amazed and appalled to realise that we now have reached the stage of handing over the care of our children to the medical profession and the State, particularly in matters which are not completely medical but are in good part moral.'

Another GP from Cornwall thanked Mr Freud for his 'wonderful support of Mrs Gillick' before making his point:

'It is a sad world when people of our age in the guise of kindness and liberality thrust children into the tensions and agonies of early adulthood long before they are ready, and rob them forever of the carefree happy years of childhood.'

Whilst a lady Doctor from Twickenham gave it to him 'hot and strong'. No doubt in her mind!

'All parents, Catholic and others, are so grateful to you for presenting a petition on behalf of Mrs Victoria Gillick. She only wants what every thinking parent wants. Our tin gods of Doctors (I am one) do far too much thinking in a negative way. The DHSS has been high-handed and not for the first time.

The parents of today, God knows, have enough trouble with their children, besides doctors perhaps adding to it. Confidentiality between doctors and teenage pipsqueaks, my foot! They, the teenagers and the doctors, think that they know it all. I have a daughter myself, happily married, who was never on the Pill and who never indulged in covert or overt "sex". Still, I can remember her at 11, 12 nay 18 years and she knew it all, all the time. Now she has 2 babies

63

and they have taught her that she never did and now does not, know it all!'

A personal touch from a Nuneaton chemist:

'I agree wholeheartedly with Mrs Gillick's stand against the General Medical Council's document about consent for prescribing the contraceptive pill for girls under 16. I would want to know if any under-age daughter of mine had the need to seek out the pill.'

I remember a few years ago, a doctor's receptionist telling me just how meaningless this sacred oath of 'confidentiality' was in practice. As she pointed out so obviously, both the receptionist and the prescribing chemist know in detail, exactly who is taking the Pill. In her small town, the parent was the only one amongst them who *didn't* know.

A school teacher wrote to Mr Freud from Cleveland:

'I am the mother of three children of 15, 13 and 11 and I teach 14–16 year old girls every working day. Mature though some of them may be, they are not old enough to take such a momentous decision – which after all is illegal. The trend for illegitimate births, abortions and the incidence of VD is inexorably upwards.

Another teacher from Swansea:

'I am convinced we do a great disservice to young people by making it seem easy, safe or normal for them to be promiscuous. I speak as one who taught eleven to nineteen year olds for thirty-two years.'

A plea from the heart came from a Bristol teacher:

'I am a mother of three children and I am a secondary school teacher. In addition I organise a "young adult" youth group.
From my constant contact with young people I know of the pressures they are under to take part in loveless sex from too early an age. Please help me to protect the youth from these false pressures. If ever our laws cease

to give protection, then we are allowing the rape of today's youth.'

A retired teacher from Kent makes her point:

'May I say how wholeheartedly I support you? I am an ex-teacher and in my experience no former pupil has finally regretted the (sensible) discipline of staff or parents – in any sphere of their lives – and some admit that they could have ruined their own lives, while too young to realise what they were doing.'

On the other side of the 'teaching coin' so to speak, came a letter from a parent in Warwickshire:

'It is high time that parents should be allowed to exercise control of their children's behaviour and not have it undermined by other people, no matter how well qualified professionally these people may be.

My own daughter was ruined by a fool of a headmistress who, without even consulting parents' wishes, let alone obtaining their consent, advised girls of fifteen and sixteen years of age how to use contraceptives. This caused disruption of our family life, and eventually has not brought my daughter any happiness. I am sure you will have the support of many parents.'

A lady from Gwent gave Freud some medical information, lest he should be ignorant of it:

'Morally it is unjustifiable for parents not to be informed. Medically no girl under sixteen should be given the pill in particular. There is a risk connected with the fusion of the epiphyses of the bones. Also, when the pill is taken by girls whose endocrine systems are immature (and this can include all girls under 20) the risks of temporary or permanent irregularity and infertility, when the pill is discontinued, are greatly increased.'

I was particularly cheered by a letter to Mr Freud from a Yorkshire grandmother. As he has five children himself, I'm sure he appreciated it:

'As a member of the silent majority may I wish you 200% success. To say more would involve writing an essay, but it is a pity the press makes such a cheap meal of Mrs Gillick's religion with accompanying murky overtones insinuated by her presumed adherence to it.

I know three 10-children families with no "problems"; I know one of 22 with financial and managing problems; I know very many 1 or 2 children families where problems are legion, both for parents and child.

As a grandmother times 4 and a recently retired SRN and health visitor, and one who has been pushed around a good deal by life, I am convinced your cause is right and essential to ultimate moral, emotional and physical survival.'

Time and again they returned to the central issue: family integrity versus state interference. A mother from Chorley was obviously speaking from experience – and one which I share with her – of trying to build a relationship of 'trust' with one's children, in the teeth of outside influences:

'From the legal point of view it would seem to be illogical to have legislation prohibiting sexual intercourse under the age of sixteen and then sanctioning the dispensing of contraceptive advice to girls who are not yet 16.

Far more worrying than that aspect, for parents of teenage girls, is the knowledge that one's daughter could consult a member of the medical profession without the parents being informed. Any caring parent who has tried to build up a relationship of trust with a daughter would find this situation extremely hurtful. Whilst much of what we see reported in the media about the attitudes and behaviour of young people today might suggest that many parents do not take seriously their responsibilities, I feel that many are concerned that their offspring still respect what might now be termed "old fashioned" moral values and they are not being supported in this task by the medical profession.'

A mother from Brighton wrote along similar lines:

'We parents are blamed for lack of control if our teenage children behave in a way detrimental to their own health and well-being, yet the control we are supposed to exercise is slowly being weakened. Allowing a GP to prescribe the contraceptive pill to a girl under 16 will erode it still further, if her parents are kept in ignorance of the fact.

When the time comes for my own daughter to seek advice about contraception, I hope she will have a word with me about it before she sits in the surgery waiting for a hard-pressed GP to scribble a prescription.'

A mother from Freud's own constituency of the Isle of Ely sent him some wise observations about the doctor/child relationship:

'This initially amounts to a conspiracy of collusion and sets the relationship between doctor and child as of more importance than that between parent and child. A doctor may leave his practice next month, but the relationship between parent and child (for good or for ill) will be of longer standing and considerable harm can result, emotionally and psychologically, when it has been damaged by this sort of "secret pact" made by an immaturely developed child and some outsider.

I do feel it is time that the status of parents, and their duties, rights and responsibilities, was once again clarified and upheld in Britain, and their authority was seen as of more permanent value to the country and their children than that of doctors, social workers and the vast number of bureaucrats who so often seem unable to cope in their own private lives but love to meddle in those of others.'

A mother wrote to him from Stockton-on-Tees:

'As a parent of three teenage girls and a member of the Mothers Union, which is concerned with the sanctity of marriage and everything that supports Christian family life, I am in support of anything that upholds the strengthening of the "family". So many aspects of life today are destroying us all morally and spiritually. The values which many condemn as "old fashioned" are to the rest of us the foundation of all that is good and true.

There are plenty of young people not sleeping around who have high ideals, but whose principles make it very difficult for them to feel "normal" in the present normal climate. They need our *trust* and support. So, on this issue as a mother, I feel it is my responsibility to know exactly *what* my doctor is prescribing for my children, and more important, *WHY*?'

Three letters from parents, who gave vent to their fears about the future of our society. The first was from Leeds:

'At the present time this country has one of the highest divorce rates in Europe, thousands of babies are being aborted each year and now the Court seeks to take away the right of a mother to guide, protect and teach her children to be loving, caring and responsible adults. The whole fabric of society is being gradually torn away, and I fear for the future of a country where children are exploited by adults to satisfy their own needs, whatever they may be.'

The second letter from Letchworth:

'It is a sad, sad world that has sunk so low in the natural world that such a petition becomes necessary. Where is the world of the human spirit and our willpower that can overcome evil?

Our children, as always, copy their elders and look to them for example. Do not our MPs, teachers and the media need to look at what they are putting forward as an example for living? Everyone starts out an innocent baby.'

The last was from a father in Surrey. His anguish was very apparent:

'I do not intend detailing the pros and cons of this issue, with which you must already be familiar. But I do want to say how urgent it is for the great, silent (and I feel right-thinking) majority to be relieved, as much as possible, of the feeling of helplessness under which they now suffer. The only people who can help are those like yourself at Westminster. It is so important that the great, moral issues do not go by default. The whole nation has the right to know the identity of persons and bodies so dedicated to freeing the young of all restraint and discipline, to their ultimate detriment. If only one of the old prophets could rise again! Or shall we say, perhaps, that "the word of the Lord came to Clement Freud?" If only the deathly silence of those people meaning well could be broken.'

Perhaps as a result of such letters as these, Mr Freud may at last have felt a tiny twinge of guilt, at having so much praise lavished upon his undeserving person! But even if he didn't, and even though he has remained adamantly opposed to me throughout, I think I managed to have the last laugh on this occasion (as on others), for I used the opportunity of these 'Freudian slips' which he sent me, to write to each of them and asked if they would like to take part in the Public Petition for their area. Most of them did, I'm glad to say.

Towards the end of the Autumn of 1983 a rather marvellous thing happened. A petitioner in London, who had been doing sterling work gathering support from amongst the Jewish, Anglican and Catholic communities, contacted the headquarters of the Salvation Army. Before very long the Salvationists themselves wrote to me, and so began my long overdue education in the history and work of the Army, and its own crusade 100 years ago, on a variety of social issues. Not least among these was their fight to outlaw the corruption of young girls in the 'white slave traffic', of child prostitution.

What had happened in the last century was this. After the Napoleonic Wars in Europe, venereal disease had broken out wholesale amongst the military (a not uncommon phenomenon in any age). In an attempt to control this epidemic, many European countries had introduced Police Regulations which allowed any women out on the streets (innocent of prostitution or otherwise) to be picked up and arrested, forced to undergo a horrendously primitive medical examination and if she refused to comply, she could be summarily convicted by a magistrate and forced to do hard labour in a camp. This was supposed to curb the spread of the disease.

In England, which was also suffering the after-effects of war, our Parliament introduced similar draconian measures under the 'Contagious Diseases Act', around the 1860s. Twenty years on, and the disease was more rampant than ever! What was worse, the Act had the effect of virtually legalising prostitution, whilst penalising women, through this medical coercion and imprisonment without trial. That was when Josephine Butler (a well-educated, middle class, vicar's wife and mother of four) and the Salvation Army stepped in. They saw how the poor and the vulnerable were suffering under this unjust régime. With prostitution flourishing, younger and younger women were being caught up in its corrupting web, unable to find an escape route out. Desperately poor families were selling their children into brothels, and the wealthy grew fatter, upon the sale of these children, to brothels and their ugly customers overseas, mainly in Europe. Hence the term 'white slave' trade.

Josephine and the 'Sally Anns', as they are affectionately known, fought long and hard against this tyranny against women and the exploitative nature of the men and women controlling them. But with the Law fixed firmly against them, they spent many anguished years campaigning, before reform eventually came. They had to convince Parliament that the intervention of the State was only making matters that much worse. They had to show that in a country professing civil liberty to its subjects, it was unjust to punish the sex who were the victims of a vice, and leave unpunished the sex who were the main cause of the vice and its dreaded consequences. They argued that such a system of medication, at the behest of the State, made the 'path of evil more easy to our sons', and the whole of the youth of England, inasmuch as (and here is the parallel with our own times) 'a moral restraint is withdrawn the moment the State recognises, and provides convenience for, the practice of a vice which it thereby declares to be necessary and venial'.

The 'Womens Revolt', as it came to be known also pointed out that:

> 'The advocates of the system have utterly failed to show, by statistics or otherwise that these Regulations have in any case, after several years' trial, and when applied to one sex only, diminished disease, reclaimed the fallen, or improved the general morality of the country.'

They went on to say that:

> 'We hold that we are bound, before rushing into experiments of legalising a revolting vice, to try to deal with the *causes* of the evil, and we dare to believe, that with wiser teaching and more capable legislation, those causes would not be beyond control.'

After seventeen years of struggle, these brave women and the Salvationists finally achieved their aims; and the brutal law was repealed; the age of consent was raised from 12 years to 16; free VD hospitals were established and the education of poor women began.

So if anyone asks me if I want to see a return to the values of Victorian England, I ask them 'Which half of her reign do you mean – the first or the second?'

That was in 1885, exactly a century ago, when Parliament in the 19th century introduced unjust regulations to doctors in an attempt to curb VD. The DHSS in the 20th century introduced guidelines in 1974, to doctors, in an attempt to curb teenage pregnancies. They failed a century ago to improve matters – just as they are failing today. The parallels are too close to be merely coincidental.

Like Josephine and the Victorian women, mothers today know all too well, that what we need in our present state of sexual delinquency is 'wiser teaching' – and wiser parents! Children need care and protection at any age and *in* any age. They do *not* need drugs, provided free at public expense, and dispensed in secret to them by the medical profession. Hard cases need *good* laws – not expedient medical remedies. Let the State put its own shaky house in order before it presumes to intrude upon the territory of others.

With the Salvation Army now marching with us, every trumpet sounding, citadels up and down the country were alerted and their prayers and hard work did so much to help the Petition to a successful conclusion.

The 'Will of the People' was being exercised at long last, just because a simple opportunity was made, which enabled that Will to express itself. A great wave of energy was being exerted, quite spontaneously, from all over the country. It had to be recognised; had to be acknowledged.

One of our greatest coups came quite unexpectedly, when one Petition organiser from the Reading constituency found that his MP was a positive supporter. He was Sir Gerard Vaughan, the former Health Minister who, when in office, had been the man responsible for the DHSS guidelines we were all now so strongly opposing. I couldn't believe it! Yet here was he, prepared to state in public that his Guidelines were wrong, in that they left an exploitable loophole for the unscrupulous to creep through. It takes a brave and honest man to admit his mistakes even in private; but to do so, unequivocally, in public, makes a veritable hero of him.

So the great day arrived in October 1983, when the first batch of Petitions were to be presented in the House of Commons. I travelled down to London alone, to meet my own presenter, Sir Bernard Braine (Freud having proved immovably hostile) outside Parliament's doors. And there, amidst the hurly burly of press photographers and maniacal London traffic, we were suddenly assailed by a crowd of cheering, waving folk, who pushed upon us in delighted confusion. They had just jumped off their coach, which had brought them all the way to London from St Helens on Merseyside, during the wee small hours. They had come to witness the presentation by their MP of their own mighty Petition in the House.

We all hurried inside the House of Commons and

squeezed into the crowded public galleries. Crowded, because another important event was taking place there: the first reading of a Private Member's Bill to outlaw 'video nasties'.

Necks were craned over the gallery rails; everyone peering down to see what the Speaker would do as the MPs stood up to read out the Petitions and present them to the House. Would Mr Speaker allow it? Would it all fizzle out like a damp squib?

There, from the floor of the House, the Voice of the People was at last being heard, as one after another *SEVEN* Members stood up and read out the identical wording, adding their own personal comments each time, to a sizeable audience of fellow MPs.

I could hardly keep still in my seat, but was for jumping up and shouting out loud for sheer joy! It was a truly remarkable occasion, by anybody's standards. The excitement and exhilaration of all concerned was palpable.

From then on, Friday after Friday, week after week, right through until Christmas, the process was repeated before the Speaker – his Green Bag bulging after every session. It was not until after Christmas that we learned the results of all our efforts: over a *million* signatures, carried in by almost three-quarters of all MPs, a huge number of whom agreed with our case.

Yet, I shall never forget, in all my life, that first amazing day in October when we saw how an idea, hatched up in a kitchen, put together on a rickety table and carried to the four corners of the Kingdom, in five short months, became a reality at last in the Mother of Parliaments.

Nor can I forget – though perhaps I ought to, in charity – looking down upon all those familiar and unfamiliar Parliamentary figures, sitting on their long benches, and spying amongst them the well-known face of my own MP, Clement Freud, poised uncomfortably, as he witnessed all his unfortunate predictions coming to nought.

Five: 'A Medical Millstone'

'That it is at least as difficult to stay a moral infection as a physical one; that such a disease will spread with the malignity and rapidity of the Plague; that the contagion, when it has once made head, will spare no pursuit or condition, but will lay hold on people in the soundest health, and become developed in the most unlikely constitutions: is a fact as firmly established by experience as that we human creatures breathe an atmosphere. A blessing beyond appreciation would be conferred upon mankind, if the tainted, in whose weakness or wickedness these virulent disorders are bred, could be instantly seized and placed in close confinement (not to say summarily smothered) before the poison is communicable.'

Little Dorrit by Charles Dickens

In the January of 1980, before we came to live in Wisbech, I and a group of parents led a deputation to No 10 Downing Street to present a Petition to the PM from five thousand people in Suffolk. We called ourselves simply 'Parents in Suffolk', and we were asking, quite modestly we thought, for the right of parents to give written consent before contraceptives were prescribed to under-age girls, as with all other medication affecting this age group. At that time, we were opposing the earlier DHSS Guidelines, first promulgated in 1974. The new ones – a variation of the old – had not yet been published.

During the same week as our London mission, and by sheer coincidence, the BMA had published, for public viewing, their *'Handbook of Medical Ethics'*. With one accord, Fleet Street went straight to that section in it, that dwelt upon consent to *abortion*, by the under-sixteens. It followed exactly the same philosophy as the DHSS rules on contraception, i.e. if the girl refused to allow her parents to be told, a doctor and gynaecologist could carry on in secret and abort her baby; sending her home afterwards without the parents knowing what had taken place.

The media then linked the two happenings together – the Petition and the BMA Handbook – and something of a furore broke out in the Press.

I presume that many people did as I did, and wrote to the BMA, outraged that such a dangerous operation as an abortion could be performed upon a girl, without anybody at home knowing of it. To whom was the girl to turn for consolation and help when she needed it, if nobody knew what had happened to her? No social worker, health visitor, or any other person could visit her, for fear of giving the game away. The only source of comfort for the girl, who might well be suffering physically, and certainly emotionally after such a traumatic experience, was the Samaritans. Calls from post-abortion women are a common occurrence for this help group, so I am told. Feminist organisations in London have even setup special centres for such women and girls to go to, in order that they may receive help and assurance, when the inevitable sorrow and regret overwhelmed them.

The BMA's response to those like me who wrote to them was odd. At first they simply didn't reply at all, for several weeks; then, after further angry promptings they sent me (and others, I later learned) a copy of an article that had been written for the magazine of the National Association of Family Planning Doctors. The President of this organisation was Dame Josephine Barnes, who was also President of the BMA at the time. Their Committee Members were largely made up of Family Planning Association people, and the magazine was financed by a pill company, Wyeth Pharmaceuticals. Its management was later to be taken over by the British Medical Journal itself.

This article was written by a Glasgow FPA doctor,

Elizabeth Wilson. It concerned her own experience of dealing with under-age girls at their central clinic, during the first eight months of 1979. She described the circumstances surrounding the attendance of these girls aged 14 and 15 years at her clinic. Eighteen of this latter age group were all 'straightforward requests for contraception' as she put it, before adding that 'The Pill was prescribed for nearly all, although in eleven cases it was known that this was without their parents' knowledge.'

I mulled over this particular article for some months, before writing to Dr Wilson herself. It had so frequently been implied, and even stated categorically by some, that those parents who were not informed of their daughter's request, were somehow bad parents, indifferent or uncaring. But if that was the case, I argued with myself, then why should anyone feel the need to keep the information secret from them? Uncaring parents would presumably welcome someone else lifting the burden of responsibility from their shoulders; they would be only too happy to have their daughters on the Pill, if they thought it might mean that they had a quiet life thereafter.

If some parents were being deliberately kept in the dark, it could only mean one thing: they *DID* care. To check my theory out, I wrote to Dr Wilson and asked why the parents were not told, in those eleven cases? Her reply was as follows:

'Dear V M Gillick   28.10.80
I am sorry I have been so long in replying to your letter of 22.8.80. It would not be possible to answer most of your queries with regard to those particular cases without a considerable amount of extra work (in extracting the case notes and reviewing them again) and in any case the amount of detail recorded by individual doctors in different cases is very variable! However, as far as I can recollect the seven with parental knowledge were all accompanied by a parent or brought a note from one. Of the 11 others (without parental knowledge) this was at the request of the

girl – in a few this was specifically religious but was more often on "old fashioned" grounds. "My dad would scalp me" or 'My mum would cast it up' (a frequent comment usually based on the experience of an older sibling).

In my personal, fairly extensive experience with this age group, the youngsters who ask for contraception are more mature, have thought out their beliefs and discussed them with their partners far more coherently than the other under 16's we see who are, or think they are, pregnant.

The contraceptive seekers are very often concerned with protecting their parents – "they would be so upset if I got pregnant", "My mum isn't strong and she couldn't cope", "They can't help not being able to understand", and I think these comments are genuine and not excuses in most instances.

Many of the youngsters attend together and the boys show a great deal of concern and often ask more questions about the side effects of the Pill than the girls.

There are two reasons why they sometimes ask that their GPs are not informed: (1) Because of his religious beliefs which they think (sometimes correctly) might lead to their parents being informed; (2) more commonly because the receptionist is personally known to the family and is known to be indiscreet.

I hope these comments are of some help. I would very much like to know whether your interest is general or professional and, if so, in what field?

Yours sincerely

E S B Wilson MB

Senior Medical Officer,

A friend of a friend of mine also received a copy of Dr Wilson's article from the BMA and had also written to her afterwards. Apparently this mother had written that, as a Christian, she would hope that no doctor would deliberately keep such information secret from her. She sent me Dr Wilson's reply, dated 23 December 1980. The two last paragraphs of that letter are, to me, the most telling:

'The girl is a person in her own right and is not the property of her parents. Her views and her right to privacy must be respected by her medical advisor. Of course the reasons for her refusal to involve her parents must be enquired into and where possible she is encouraged to confide, but ultimately the decision to have sexual intercourse is hers and her partner's.

I am not sure of the relevance of Christianity to the principles involved – children do not always subscribe to the religious views of their parents and a Muslim mother would presumably feel as strongly as you do and still have no right to compel her daughter to accept her beliefs.'

I make no comment upon these letters, except to observe, that when I actually met Dr Elizabeth Wilson earlier this year, after a Tyne Tees television programme on teenage sex, I found her singularly insensitive to the feelings of young people. We were sitting with a group of other adults, refreshing ourselves with wine and sandwiches after the show, and discussing the subject in greater depth. Two teenage girl 'buskers' who had also been on the programme were at our table. They were bright young things in jolly clothing, and full of beans. Suddenly Dr Wilson turned to them, opened her handbag and proceeded to produce a sample of an Intra Uterine Device which she then proceeded to tell these girls all about. She never once noticed their obvious repugnance to such an inappropriate gesture. 'What on earth have you got there?' I asked, laughing incredulously. 'For goodness sake, put it away! We don't want to have to look at that sort of thing.' Hastily she replaced the bent bit of copper wire in her bag, and shortly afterwards left. The two girls were thoroughly put off by the whole, bizarre episode, and said after she had gone that they thought contraception of that sort looked horrid, and they thought the Pill was dangerous as it affected every cell in your body with hormones. So I told them about natural family planning doctors, and they seemed to think that was a much healthier idea altogether!

As that teacher once wrote to me: 'And how little do

they seem to understand the young . . . . '

The immediate reaction to receiving Dr Wilson's letter, was to alert me to the fact that there were some doctors in birth control practice, who were not only amoral, but even deeply hostile towards those possessing a religious faith of any kind.

So often we hear clinic doctors expressing the opinion that they are not there to 'preach morality' to the young. It isn't their job to do so, they say. Yet most of them are extremely moralistic about a girl or women who smokes when pregnant or on the Pill. They admonish them, tell them they are socially irresponsible, etc. Yet if they care as much as they say about a girl's health in matters of smoking, why are they so morally shut-mouthed when it comes to the far greater and immediate risks, associated with the Pill and early sex?

The answer is probably because huge publicity, especially by the BMA, against smoking generally and of women on the Pill in particular, has made doctors aware of the dangers and ready to speak out about it, knowing that they will not be branded as 'puritans' or 'old fashioned'.

Besides which, those doctors whose sole career is centred around contraception, are hardly likely to be the first to sound the warning bell on particular forms of birth control, having been prescribing them to unsuspecting clients for years.

That kind of evidence has always come from researchers *outside* the prescribing fraternity or the drugs industry. In the same way, tobacconists or cigarette manufacturers are never the ones to warn customers to stop smoking – it would hardly be in their best interests to do so!

Perhaps it is also true that, just because these specialised birth control clinics do not have to deal with the unfortunate results of some of their prescribing, that they are often regarded by GPs as only 'part time' doctors. When you consider that a family doctor has to have regard to the *whole* of their patients' lives, their medical history, hereditary factors, their environment, personality and family relationships; in short their past and long-term future health and welfare, then you can understand their concern about these other 'outside' agents, dealing secretly with their own patients.

It may well be that such specialised clinics provide a wider choice of contraceptive methods and more experts to apply them, and may even guarantee a greater degree of secrecy to the young; but are they really the most suitable source of advice for schoolchildren, either ethnically or even practically?

An example of what can unfortunately happen, when the 'right hand doesn't know what the left hand is doing' came in a personal article by a GP in a medical magazine this year.

This particular practitioner related how a 14 year old girl patient of his had visited him with a note from a Family Planning Clinic. The girl was the eldest of three children in a one-parent family. The note from the clinic explained how the child had been put on the Pill by them and had returned later on with low abdominal pains, which the clinic doctor thought might be due to pelvic inflammatory disease. They suggested in the note to the GP that he give her a course of antibiotics after a high vaginal swab.

The GP was appalled that such a young child should be on the Pill. He was equally surprised that the clinic had not taken the swab themselves though he himself would not do such a thing without the parents' consent. He questioned the girl and gave her an abdominal examination, finally referring her to the next available gynaecological clinic, attaching the FP note to his own referral letters.

On looking at her medical notes after she had left, he noticed that only two months earlier the girl had consulted his partner with an 'Episode of haemoptysis'. An X-ray at the time failed to reveal any pathology and the condition had not recurred.

What gave both GPs the greatest concern, was that his partner had never suspected that the child was on the Pill, and that she might even have been suffering from a pulmonary embolism. The clinic had informed *no one* of their prescribing to her.

As the GP wrote in the article, it was a terrible state of

affairs, now that doctors in future would have to ask all young girls with pains in their chests, if they were on the Pill!

'Confidentiality' is of course at the heart of the dilemma in such cases. It is supposed by some to be an immutable law, almost sacred, even by those who find religion obnoxious in all other ways!

A London GP exploded the myth of confidentiality when he wrote to me, giving an example of how 'confidentiality' could be set aside in certain circumstances:

> 'Confidentiality, as you know, is a warm subject with most doctors. It is, however, not absolute and you may have seen in the *Handbook of Medical Ethics* of the BMA that under Advice to Armed Forceds Medical Officers 2.20 (p. 21) it states "a patient who consults a medical officer in the Services should be aware that the duty of the doctor to keep secret the information given to him is importantly modified". It goes on to say that there are times when a doctor is obliged to discuss cases with his commanding officers in the interest of the unit as a whole. Now it may be said that the common good, regarded in this instance as the efficient functioning of the unit, requires such a course. This argument might regard the good of the unit as superior to that of the individual.
>
> The contrary view, however, is that the good of the family in society equates to that of the unit in the Services.'

Earlier this year, following the success of the Appeal Court Ruling before Christmas 1984, a family planning doctor wrote to me from Surrey. She was extremely hostile to the 3 Judges' Ruling (although in common with many others, she saw it as *my* Ruling and not the Judges'). She wrote:

> 'I think you have no idea how destructive and thoughtless you are. Of course we understand your feelings as a mother about girls of under 16 and the Pill.

Unfortunately you have failed to take into account the deprived children.

As family planning doctors, this group is one of our special cases. You have made their lot infinitely worse. They are looking, outside the home, for the affection they lack at home. They hope to find it in a sexual relationship. This we regret but cannot alter.

Thanks to you we are not now even permitted to give them advice about any form of birth control. Instead they come to us about a termination of pregnancy.

I recently saw an under 16 girl whose parents had deserted her. She was frightened of her legal guardian. Naturally she was having a sexual relationship and desperately needed advice. I was the only adult she could talk to. There are many like her. You are preventing these children from getting help. Neither you nor I can prevent them from having sex.

Please stop congratulating yourself – anyone with compassion and experience in this field knows that what you have done is a disaster to young people with inadequate or uncaring parents.'

Is this attitude typical of birth-controllers? Do they all give themselves pats on the back for their 'compassion and experience'? Is 'regret' and several months supply of a hormone drug the best they can offer a child in distress? Do any of them ever trouble to leave their surgeries and go home-visiting once in a while? When an emotionally insecure child falls foul of her contraceptive therapy or contracts a nasty disease, or is abandoned by her sexual partner or her relations, is there nothing more that these clinic specialists can do for her – except pass her back to her GP or others to cure and care for her? Their 'compassion' seems only word thin; their care measures only the distance between the prescription pad and the clinic door. Is it fair, is it just, that a child deprived of parental love should also be deprived of her health, through expedient medication?

A general practitioner from Cornwall seems to have heard all the 'old arguments' for pills before:

'Of course all the old arguments are now being trotted

out once more, but your remark about "second rate expedients" sums it up in a nutshell! Likewise Dr Adrian Rogers' statement that with proper care and guidance, prescribing the Pill to problem teenagers is unnecessary.

When, oh when, will people learn that no problem is solved by clipping away at the edges! Until we get to the heart of the matter and turn round this permissive society to logic and commonsense, nothing will be resolved.

But you have won a marvellous victory. Now I feel secure in continuing my stand in support of you without fear of litigation (not that a court case would alter my stance in any way whatsoever), but it is rather appalling that a doctor could be struck off by the GMC for telling parents.'

Put simply again by a Yorkshire GP:

'We see the present trends as the result of activities by misguided "progressives" and a recipe for untold misery with far-reaching effects.'

Actually, I call them '*re*gressives' – taking us backwards into the epidemics of social disease, common enough in the last century.

No doctor worth his salt ever treats his patients flippantly, certainly not when they are only children. A Lancashire GP gave his experience of dealing with such cases:

'As a family doctor I am acutely aware of the problem and have had occasions when I have experienced great difficulty in arriving, with the patient, at what was hoped was the correct answer. Each and every case is different but I cannot myself accept that treatment of a minor for any condition without the parents' knowledge can ever be the right course of action, and the greater the emotional overlay, the greater is the need for parental involvement.

The use of the pill is too often thought of in the

simple terms of contraception, and the wider implications of increased risk of venereal disease and the emotional trauma of increasingly casual sex are overlooked. In my opinion there are few – if any – girls under the age of sixteen who are mature enough to handle these pressures on their own.

I have discussed this issue with many of my colleagues and I can tell you that to date I have yet to meet one who disagrees with the stand you have taken. Let us hope that you have started something which will fasten momentum as the full implications of Justice Woolf's pronouncement are realised.'

A Buckingham GP gives his views on the GMC Ruling:

'I would, as a GP and parent, like to express my support for your case against the DHSS and its recent recommendations with regard to the treatment of minors. I have been alarmed not only by this but by the decision of the GMC that a doctor might have to justify a decision to discuss with a minor's parents the outcome of a consultation, to the Disciplinary Committee, should such a discussion be held against the minor's expressed wishes.

My interpretation of this situation is that the GMC is attempting to set itself above the law and against the moral framework within which I have been brought up and trained.'

Notice how a *GP* is not afraid to tackle the word 'moral' in relation to his judgements; whereas a birth-control specialist abjures it. The GMC *et al* came under fire again from a Hertfordshire GP:

'While I don't believe everyone should have 10 children, I support your efforts generally. I am not RC. The GMC ethics booklet and the BMA advice are both bad and I have no intention of treating children under 16 without parental knowledge whatever they advise or instruct, and *I* mean for *any* condition – emergencies excepted.

I have resigned from the BMA until they see sense.'

Brave man! But I felt his opening remarks about my multitude of children a little inappropriate! After all, if most women wanted 10 children, they would presumably have had them. As it is, most of them don't. In fact one in seven women cannot have any children at all!

With our national birthrate down to 1·6 children per woman (and this includes all those ethnic women who usually have higher birthrates) there must be a tragically large number of childless couples. Some would add that a major cause for concern is the self-induced infertility, brought about through too early and frequent sex combined with various forms of contraceptives or abortion. Others would say, ignore these causes and let's get on with *in vitro* fertilisation, test tube babies and all the rest. Medical thought processes are sometimes difficult to follow.

'Of course the modern doctor may only have become one because he's clever and may have no idea of ethics or philosophy,' wrote a consultant from Harley Street. Perhaps that would be better applied to medical research technicians than doctors. They seem to be the ones making all the running these days.

Some doctors seem to resent the slur upon their profession, which medical authorities have encouraged. A doctor from Bristol writes:

'I just wanted to say how delighted I am to see someone make a stand on this contraceptive issue. I am constantly ashamed of the title "doctor" these days. You are doing more for world peace with your support for the family than a hundred Bruce Kents. Please don't give up.'

In 1983 many doctors wrote to me, deeply disturbed at Judge Woolf's decision. For some it was a question of law, as with this Sussex GP's wife:

'I hope you will receive hundreds (thousands) of letters supporting you in your fight against "Big Brother" as reported in the press.

I cannot understand how the doctors have got away

with it up till now (my husband is a retired GP). After all, they are encouraging someone to break the law. I have read today's paper and the judge is playing with words I feel. If the law is being ignored with the connivance of judges then the law should be changed.

It is nice to know there are still people with ''fire in their bellies'' about! I hope the matter does not rest now, but that some definite ruling will come out of it all eventually.'

From a Hampshire doctor came this thought:

'It has been decreed that until the age of 16 children need the guidance and consent of their parents to participate in such activities as are legally permitted to them. They may not smoke, drink alcohol, place bets, drive cars or engage in sexual intercourse. The law is quite clear on these points.

As doctors we would be failing in our duty if we encourage, condone or conspire with them to break the law. As parents we should guide and inspire our children to uphold the law, and thereby develop them into the next generation of responsible citizens.'

A Glasgow doctor takes the argument further. Note his comments on BMA procedures:

'For months, I have been meaning to write to you, to tell you of my strong support of your efforts to stop under-age girls receiving the contraceptive pill, without their parents' consent. I consider this is a dangerous precedent in depriving people of their just rights. It puzzles me that the males involved with these under-age girls are never brought to law. There is a law to protect them.

I am a member of the BMA, but I have never been asked my views on the subject of under-age contraception – nor have any of my colleagues in the BMA as far as I know.'

Yet it must have irked BMA members, to see all their hard earned subscription fees being spent so wantonly on glossy four-page Parliamentary Briefings, whilst they themselves received nothing but a cursory ruling in the *Handbook of Medical Ethics*.

A doctor from Surrey asked a very important question. It was a central point in the Appeal Court's deliberations in 1984:

> 'What would happen if I were to prescribe "the pill" for a ward without the Court's knowledge – let alone permission? I think that we would find the Court reserved to itself the very rights it denies to parents, though both parents and the Court bear the same responsibility for children in their respective care.'

A Hertfordshire doctor, having said his piece about the BMA, made a lively plea for the dignity of women:

> 'I don't know if you see the BMJ (British Medical Journal) but recent letters from GPs have launched devastating attacks on the position adopted by the BMA in this matter, a position which one can only describe as being based on trendy thinking.
>
> It is so encouraging also to see Germaine Greer thinking the unthinkable and saying the unsayable. She has a great capacity for broad and original thinking. No doubt you saw her description of the convent school in Australia. She says some of the nuns think she may end up a saint. Essentially her message is that women should stop colluding with their own devaluation, by present cultural stereotypes of women.
>
> It is so refreshing to see women like yourself cutting through the mess, muddle and mindless recourse to sexuality as a kind of social drug, which idea befuddles the mind of our so-called professionals and legislators.'

Doctors, like the rest of us, feared and resented the way in which the almighty State appears to be taking over our lives, and the decisions we make about ourselves and our families. A doctor's wife from Worcestershire wrote:

> 'My husband and I have followed with great interest your attempt in the High Court to get a declaration

against the DHSS on their "contraceptive" memorandum. We have just heard in stunned disbelief, on the 1.00 pm news that you have failed to achieve this objective. We know from our work that this is the tip of the iceberg, in an attempt by the state to erode the authority and responsibility of parents and we view the attitude of the DHSS in these matters with grave misgiving.'

Again a lady doctor from Gwent, on this aspect of the argument:

'It is totally unacceptable for a situation to exist where, in effect, the State decides on the moral behaviour of a child under age, regardless of the wishes of the parents. If a parent inflicts injury on a child he is rightly condemned and taken to court; but if a parent seeks to bring up a child in the "nurture and admonition of the Lord" he may be overruled. This Ruling is a further step in the undermining of the family and needs to be resisted.'

One might also add to that, that if a parent does (wilfully or otherwise) neglect his children, the doctors involved in the wardship proceedings usually have a whole file of evidence against the parents. But if a parent has a grievance against a doctor, who wilfully or otherwise assists the moral corruption of their child, it is well nigh impossible to get evidence against him at all.

The insidious nature of this State 'take-over' and the way in which medical personnel have indirectly encouraged it, was examined by a Northern Ireland hospital consultant, who wrote:

'For many years the authority of parents has been eroded by those who claim to act in the child's interest; although I have never known of a case in my own hospitals (and I worked for years in a children's hospital in England) the medical profession has sought authority through the Courts to treat children against the wishes of their parents. This authority has been granted on occasions where treatment was said to be life-saving.

Unfortunately the principle became established that the medical profession could overrule parents in circumstances where it (the profession) considered the child's life was endangered.

It was therefore a simple step for the DHSS to decree that teenage girls had a right to contraceptive advice and supplies even against the wishes of their parents; and in this way the DHSS has encouraged promiscuity among the young. Those of us who take a responsible moral attitude can but deplore this development.'

Just how true his words were can be seen by the way in which a birth-control agent in 1985 had even gone to the lengths of having a child made a Ward of Court in order that an abortion could be carried out upon her, and contraceptives given, against the parents' wishes; the argument being that a pregnancy was endangering her life. The contraceptives apparently were not, nor the sexual acts by the male involved. Who were the beneficiaries of that sorry affair: the mother? . . . . the girl? . . . . the unborn child? . . . . *OR* only the young man and the abortion agency?

A stark reminder of how such policies, once adopted by the medical profession, can eventually lead to a denial of the doctor's *own* freedom of conscience, came in a letter from America, from an Eastern European refugee anaesthetist:

'I read the article about your struggle against contraceptives in *The Times* of July 20, 1983; at that time I was in Cyprus (Nicosia) where I fled to the West from a tourist trip for my religious belief.

I am a Czechoslovak doctor and, since I refused to administer anaesthesia to patients undergoing artificial interruption of normal pregnancies, I was degraded. I could expect only inferior posts in the future. Therefore I emigrated. I arrived in the USA a week ago.

God is on our side, be strong! I am sending to you a copy of a medical article on contraception showing deleterious effects of contraceptives. Thus, you will be prepared also to argue with doctors. The author tries to show also the positive effects; however, he cannot deny the harmful effects. Please, ask a doctor-believer for explaining you the parts of the text which are difficult to understand.

May God help you! I admired your courage, Mrs Gillick! Mr Gillick surely encouraged you.'

Plenty of doctors were already supplying me with all the information on 'side-effects' already. A lady doctor from Yorkshire wrote:

'It is inadvisable to prescribe "the pill" before full maturity is established. Not all menstruation is associated with ovulation which is motivated by the pituitary gland.

There is a suggestion that there is a connection between early and promiscuous sexual intercourse and cancer of the cervix and breast. "AIDS" is said to be associated with illicit and casual intercourse.'

A Manchester doctor explained even further:

'It is surely odd that one cannot act against even the dangerous and unhealthy appendix, but one can now use a powerful hormone against the healthy pituitary and ovary, even in direct opposition to the parent. Also the so-called "pill" is itself suspect; there is strong reason to suspect it can cause deep thrombosis; it is suspected of possible links with later development of malignancy. But the major point is that parental consent is required for life-saving procedures, but it is now declared lawful to expose the healthy organs of a minor to powerful agents.

There is a drug, cyproterone, which acts by a rather different mechanism on the *male* reproductive system; as I, and my colleagues, understand it we may not prescribe it even to adults without full explanations to the patient, and his written consent is advisable. May we now suppose this drug can be prescribed to male

90

minors without parental consent? If not, is not an illegal sex discrimination approached?

If a minor does in fact develop thrombosis, perhaps fatal, what is the position of the prescriber in the face of any civil action for damages? Would the recent ruling be an effective defence?'

The Pill itself came again under fire from two Surrey doctors:

'I can think of no other drug which would have survived this long without being deleted by the Committee on Safety of Medicines. When I think of the reasons that Butazolidin was removed after being on the market for 35 years, they are positively miniscule by comparison with the oral contraceptive. As Dr Sugrue pointed out, the immature cervix does not stand a chance when exposed to drugs of this nature. It is common medical knowledge that early sexual exposure predisposes to genital cancer and I am at a loss to understand present medical teaching and attitudes on this matter.'

The other doctor wrote:

'I am in no doubt the Pill will go down in history as the greatest medical disaster ever. It is a crime against women – mostly inspired by men – they won't take it themselves.'

But perhaps it is the philosophy that came with the Pill which is the 'greatest medical disaster': The profound belief that pregnancy is in itself a kind of *disease*, to be avoided at all costs; and the suffering caused by contraceptive methods is said to be infinitely preferable to the horror of an unexpected attack of fecundity. Women *must* suffer the unfortunate 'side-effects' of the Pill because women are the source of the 'pregnancy-disease'; they are carriers of it, and must be controlled in the interests of a deeply alarmed society!

Any woman found resisting this treatment altogether

must be scorned and made to feel a social outcast by one and all. She is a reactionary, a subversive, and no friend of Caesar's, or his medical minions.

The Hippocratic Oath is rather scoffed at by modern medics. None of them took it. It has no relevance to medical practice these days. Even its updated version, as outlined in the Charter of Medicine of the BMA, which was formulated in 1947 after the awful revelations of the Nuremberg trials, has no bearing upon present birth-control methods. For the Charter stated that the primary duty of a doctor was to care for humanity; and the gravest crime was to co-operate in 'suicide, murder or abortion'.

Yet within twenty years of that declaration, in 1967, abortion had been licenced; and confidentiality had become so distorted a principle, that this 'gravest crime' could be committed upon a mere girl, without even her parents' knowledge. Some doctors and nurses find it all too much to stomach. A nurse from Middlesex wrote:

'Having worked considerably, over the past twenty odd years, in gynaecology, I was extremely shocked about five years ago to learn that an apparently responsible consultant performed termination of pregnancy on such a young person in secrecy, i.e. the mother who brought her daughter to hospital was totally deceived. I must be frank and admit that this is the only case I actually know – but then, I had never queried the possibility!'

A few years ago the editorial of one medical journal posed the rhetorical question that, since schoolgirl mothers were something 'society does not want' shouldn't they receive *compulsory* abortions? A logical conclusion under a Tyranny perhaps, but not *here*, in Great Britain, surely?

Despite the apparent collapse of basic medical ethics as enshrined in BMA and DHSS manifestos, most conscientious doctors have an instinctive grasp of what is moral and right, even if they are not always permitted to exercise their ethical judgement.

A doctor and his wife from Sussex wrote to Clement Freud on just such moral dilemmas:

'We are writing about doctors giving contraceptive advice and the Pill to girls under 16. Since pregnancy is not of itself an illness but has moral implications not normally found in illnesses, two special factors must be considered by doctors:

1. Extra-marital intercourse is in Christian teaching morally wrong in God's sight, and thus doctors who encourage others to practice it aid and abet wrong behaviour.

2. It is parents who are responsible for their children, and doctors have no right to withhold details from them let alone to encourage their children in immoral behaviour.'

To which honest protest, our DHSS might cry 'Oh, who will rid me of these troublesome Christians!'

Yet even family-planners have 'mavericks' within their ranks. Such a one wrote to me from Cambridgeshire:

'The health and propaganda elements in the debate are what concern me. Young adolescents are very vulnerable to pressures which seem to offer ''freedom'' but in reality are a manipulation of their normal desires.

It is this aspect which has always concerned me. Doctors have been ''trapped'' by the media and other manipulators and are usually not themselves aware or interested in this aspect.'

Again Freud received sound warnings from a medical man from Nottingham:

'As a general practitioner I am well aware of the human situations encountered, but believe that we ignore moral principles at our peril, and must stem the surge of pressures encouraging sex without responsibility and murder of the unseen for convenience. This cannot be the way forward for society.'

A retired consultant radiologist from Gloucestershire wrote in the same vein, on a number of points:

'It inevitably undermines parental autonomy. This is currently at a very low ebb, with disastrous results for society. Whatever protests are made, the current legislation has the effect of seeming to give official sanction, if not actual encouragement of promiscuity, to an especially vulnerable age group.

'It appears to be prompted by the currently disastrous attitude of giving short-term expediency priority over morality. It encourages small pressure groups in the medical profession and allied folk, to think they can dictate ethics at the expense of wider social responsibility. In any case the subject has never been widely debated by the profession, although the implication has been put about that it has been.

In conclusion, this whole situation is directed at a small minority of children and parents at the expense of the vast majority of responsible parents. Hard cases make bad laws.'

Two doctors, one from Cardiff and the other from Essex, gave their experience of dealing with these 'hard cases'. The first was a woman GP and former family planner:

'I would, however, spend quite a long time always, reasoning with them – as a result I then succeeded. However, one parent tried to overrule me with the words "In this permissive age . . . etc", to which I replied "And who is being permissive – you and your husband!" How sad it is that the word "control" for male and female, young and not so young, seems to be unknown or at least unused by the young and by parents of the young.'

The second doctor expressed a point of view which many doctors still feel is a very fair one:

'I am not a Roman Catholic nor would I own to any religious belief. I am in no way opposed to contraception, but I do believe that members of my profession should not be above the law. I have long failed to understand how the medical profession can claim the right to condone and assist acts of unlawful sexual intercourse. I would go further to say it has been my policy to gently but firmly refuse any under age child, even when accompanied by a parent. In fact, to one mother I said, "Do you appreciate you are asking me to assist both you and your daughter to break the law?" Despite these considerations, under age children do attend clinics and give false information; no effort is made to verify them re. production of passport or birth certificate. I would however disagree with you that I should inform parents, because I think I should be known to be lawful and morally correct, but not to act as an informer, breaking a trust which even a child has the right to expect of my profession.'

But would he maintain this "trust" if the child was only 12 or 13 years old, I wonder? And don't parents have a right to expect that a doctor be trustworthy with *them* also? It is a difficult point. If the child was abusing himself or herself with drugs, solvent, alcohol or cigarettes, would the doctor still keep silence, and only give advice to the child?

A Hertfordshire doctor, also herself a mother, wrote to me explaining how, when her daughters were young she had:

' . . . an uphill struggle during their adolescence to instill in them the concept of the sacredness of human life and their own sense of responsibility toward their own bodies, and their future children. All too often institutions like the schools and the Marriage Guidance Bureau seemed to work all out for a purely hedonistic, nihilistic and selfish philosophy of life. You must speak for thousands of parents.'

A welcome few words of spiritual comfort came, after we had initially lost the case in 1983, from a Cambridgeshire anaesthetist:

'I am writing because it is so easy, especially in defeat, to feel that one is a lone voice, and it is important for you to know the support and the prayers that you have behind you – chiefly, of course, the words of Our Lord against those who cause His little ones to stumble. And if God is with us, who can be against us? I am not a member of the BMA because of its stance on ethical matters, but I am embarrassed by their welcoming of the judge's decision. The FPA, as an interested party, is bound to welcome it; but one would have hoped for a broader view, including the protection of the family and the rights of parents, from the BMA.

Please keep fighting the good fight, and God will give you strength.'

Society has placed a great burden upon the shoulders of the doctors. It probably has done so always; but in this age, excess of all the appetites and over indulgence in all the seven deadly sins seems to have made the ordinary family doctor's life not a happy one. For it is they who have to pick up all the broken pieces of tattered lives, expressed in the sick bodies they see: the alcoholic, glutton, bully and bullied. Now even children are coming to them with their adult sexual vices, demanding that they save them from a fate worse than abstinence.

If ever I thought that I might be over dramatising my case, and that it wasn't really as bad as all that, that naïveté has long since been dispelled. The frightening tones of those who vociferously oppose parents, and want to drive doctors into being no more than pawns in a social game of human engineering, have wakened up the public at last.

From a State Hospital in South West Africa a letter arrived in July 1983. Even over there, this unholy phenomenon can apparently be seen. The doctor wrote:

'The news of your action in the High Court has reached here, in my air mail issues of *The Times*, and I want you to know how much support you have from likeminded people.

I am a surgeon, father of eleven children, and in the process of conversion to Catholicism, but even if I were none of these, I would be on your side. You are fighting against a quite monstrous evil.'

Six: 'A Common Experience'

Most people believe that young girls are better off without having a sexual experience, whilst still at school. I say most people, because there *are* those who think that child sex is great; the paedophiles and those who pander to their unnatural desires, in some of our dirty 'dailies and Sundays'. I call these people 'literary flashers', because they write all about what the dirty-minded are thinking and doing.

They are part of the problems facing the young; no matter how earnestly they claim to be doing no more than revealing 'the shocking truth' and 'true facts' or the 'story no one else would print' – faithful to their journalistic calling, so they say. When the true, shocking fact is, that a juicy sex story always sells newspapers, no matter who it is about; and quite clearly children have now become part of that sexual market for some editors. Their hypocrisy and covert voyeurism is sickening. They say that some men go mad at forty; some of them begin reading dirty newspapers; a few of them even begin writing for them . . . . but setting aside these unhealthy or self-serving groups, we are still left with the problem of deciding what we believe constitutes the right kind of 'protection' for young girls. Parliament has legislated several times during the past 100 years to give legal protection to the young. By and large these laws reflect the commonly held view that, for girls, the sexual act was a disaster in every way. She was physically not able to endure it and would be badly damaged by prolonged or brutal intercourse. Emotionally it would disorientate her; casting her both as woman and child at the same time. Adolescence is a jerky enough time for most youngsters, without having to worry desperately about another adolescent's personal problems, as well as their own.

Morally, it sets a girl at odds with nature and society

together; since any child conceived would have no mature father or companionable siblings to protect or surround it. Moreover, children left unprotected by law or circumstance are prey to any amount of abuse, either of their unpaid labour, or their vulnerable bodies. Hard times encourage unscrupulous individuals, who exploit the weak or wayward. Only now are we beginning to realise just how dangerous it is for children in society. Sexual abuse of them within families is said to be one horrible manifestation of the present generation of adult perversions.

The fathers involved in such abuse were themselves young boys in the Swinging Sixties and earlier. Somewhere along the line, that young post-war generation lost its way completely. The confusion at the present moment lies between two conflicting ideas, yet based on the common assumption of those who hold them, that schoolgirls are indeed 'at risk'. The one faction says that girls are physically, mentally and emotionally more *mature* than thirty years or so ago, and that therefore the age of consent should now be lowered to around 14, but with contraception available to them, because they are physically, mentally and emotionally too *immature* to bear a child! The other faction says that more and more girls come from socially deprived homes with immature and irresponsible parents, and that these girls need the protection of contraception – whilst engaging in immature and irresponsible sexual relationships with equally immature and irresponsible males.

They call this the 'cycle of deprivation'; yet those who see it in action, seem hell bent on keeping it spinning at greater and greater speed, in tighter and tighter circles, with deprived children being deprived still further.

If we truly believed that young boys and girls are more mature than of yore, and that society is a more gentle, civilised and easy-going place to grow up in, then why does Parliament persist in altering the age limits of so many attractive diversions beloved of the young, on the grounds that they are trying to protect them? Take for example the buying of fireworks. Children now have to be *sixteen* before they can purchase a single, innocuous sparkler. They cannot buy a packet of cigarettes or tobacco, even for mum or dad, until sixteen. Where once a macho lad could leap on his 750 cc motorbike the day he left school, now he is reduced to beetling along on his noisy 50 cc Japanese monster. And the British motorcycle industry has all but vanished as a consequence. The school leaving age is raised to sixteen and glue is now rarely sold to any child without a note from the parents.

Are we being repressive towards the young, taking away their rights, or merely facing up to reality?

G. K. Chesterton, that master of the literary paradox, once wrote:

> 'If we wish to protect the poor we shall be in favour of fixed rules and clear dogma. The rules of a club occasionally favour the poor member. The drift of a club is always in favour of the rich.'

In such a context as ours children could be said to be the 'poorest of the poor', for they are totally dependent on the love and care of adults, for their happy welfare, spiritual as well as material.

Being born a post-war baby myself, I can well remember growing up, a confused adolescent, in the Sixties. We were the first generation to be relatively monied, with jobs and spare cash within easy reach of most teenagers.

We were also the first generation to be actively encouraged by the media establishment to treat our parents with 'dishonour', to call them foolish names and set ourselves totally apart from them. The 'generation gap' was not an idea coined by youngsters, but by those who sought to free them from the restraints of relatives and authority.

A kid on his own can be sold any number of tawdry baubles, by a clever manipulator.

Parents were just the means by which their children acquired material comfort and satisfaction. It was a free-standing right, which bore no traces of reciprocity in the young. Trust, truth and fidelity were all a one-way gift – from parent to child. But this habit, developed in us teenagers, of getting what we wanted, when we wanted it – this philosophy of 'taking the waiting out of wanting' and discarding what we didn't want, just as rapidly; this was a habit, almost impossible to break.

Now as adults and parents ourselves, many of us of that Sixties generation find it well nigh impossible to come to terms with the daily demands of our *own* children. Our children are thereby reaping what their parents sowed: selfishness.

Most children nowadays are not as materially or physically deprived as they were fifty years ago. But many are emotionally so; even more receive no spiritual sustenance whatsoever. The 'hard stones' of a consumer age, is all they have to keep the loneliness at bay – for a while at least.

Most parents nowadays mean well in what they do; but they, like their children, need help and guidance, and neither of these is forthcoming. Isn't it odd, how those who profess to hold no moral viewpoint on anything at all, are so often the ones to point the finger of recrimination at those whom they believe are acting immorally. 'Irresponsible', 'uncaring', 'delinquent' says the family planner to a colleague, when describing the parent of a child to whom they have just secretly prescribed a dangerous drug!

Perhaps their lack of faith in other people's small virtues reveals their own personal shortcomings. Yet the cumulative effect of all these killjoys of motherhood, and these counsellors of despair is to (partially at least) convince many, otherwise sensible, folk that there is really nothing that anyone can do about it.

With all these years of primary, secondary and further education behind us, we seem to have become 'technological giants and moral pygmies', bereft of new ideas from amongst the very people to whom we have traditionally turned for wise advice and inspired leadership: the educators, the churches, the politicians.

Instead, they either throw up their hands in horror or throw in the sponge in defeat. When those with all the benefits of education and training back off from their social and moral responsibilities towards their less fortunate brethren, that is when the old Nanny State moves in to run the show.

But the 'State' is not concerned with personal liberty, far less personal morality. The State is, by its own nature and requirements essentially impersonal, secular, utilitarian and cost-conscious.

The DHSS guidelines on 'Adolescent Fertility Management', to give it the official title, is a classic example of this. The primary concern of this departmental maxim is to prevent teenage pregnancies: nothing more and nothing less. If contraceptives are considered to be the most up-to-date method of achieving this aim, then their distribution amongst teenagers, from the onset of puberty, must be facilitated. Morality doesn't come into it (neither does the law, apparently!). If *more* pregnancies seem to result at the same time, don't worry about it, just keep ploughing on regardless. If the *idea* was a good one, ignore the consequences – stick with the *idea*. Their logic is as immutable as the Mad Hatter's and just as exasperating.

The machinery of the State, unlike any other human institution, or business even, is utterly incapable of voluntarily changing course, or accepting 'alteration when it alteration finds'. Unless and until other forces, outside its compass, oblige it to do so, the State is impervious to reason or entreaty.

A letter from a hostile Fife schoolteacher is redolent of this State mentality: judgemental, yet basically ill-informed and amoral.

'You describe the "other side" of the argument as a "council of despair" and up to a point you are right. It must be, of necessity, in the case of these young people who have, for one reason or another embarked on a sexual career. As a teacher in secondary school I am aware of *many* pregnancies *each year* to girls under 16 and I am well aware of the thinking process or lack of it – the psychological background which gives rise to it.

It is of course too trite to say – and it is in itself erroneous – that more contraceptives *lead to* more abortions; they are both symptoms. I can look at the casual relationship more dispassionately, through not being a parent myself and not having an esoteric code of moral dogma to confuse my vision.

When you suggest that young people need protecting from themselves you must follow the logic of your own statement. The principal danger is pregnancy. Cervical cancer etc. is an issue which should be addressed, but my understanding is that it stems from promiscuity/lack of hygiene etc., rather than sexual experience *per se*. Most cancers are, in any case, psychological and emotional in origin, even when there may be an environmental trigger.

When a young person goes behind her parents' back it is a symptom that the relationship *has already* broken down. If parents had to be told, it would lead, to my certain knowledge and experience, to physical violence and to young people being thrown out of their houses with nowhere to go.

A point which was made, but not strongly enough, is that parents can be purely incompetent – not in any "physical" sense (i.e. the children are clothed, fed, kept clean etc) – but emotionally so, and it is utterly politically impossible for these people to be relieved of their duties: (a) there are far too many of them; (b) who is to judge the incompetence? (c) they would object too strongly! I can see that you have just no idea about millions of "ordinary" parents who are just hopeless! I mean, why do you think they have children in the first place? It is a reaction to their own emotional weaknesses (not *everyone* of course!!).

What I would like to know is this: If your child when, say, 13, got contraceptive facilities and you were told, exactly what would you do? How would you react? Are you *sure* that your reactions would be correct? How can you be so sure?

I absolutely agree that there was a *problem* with "child prostitution" etc., in Victorian days, but I wonder if the apparent immediate solution – repression – actually proved a long-term benefit to these girls or to women generally who continued generally repressed for very many decades in so many ways. What was really needed at that time was a radical new deal for all sorts of women. Paradoxically, dealing dramatically with one particular manifestation of their subservient position, actually *put off* the day when the general position would be addressed.

Parents have, or should have, few rights. By their choice of parenthood they take on many responsibilities. One of these is to create a family atmosphere where their children will want and will feel able to bring to them their problems. If they fail in this they must allow their children the option of choosing someone else to confide in.

I challenge you to a serious and deep debate.'

What worried me most about that letter, was that this fellow was actually *in loco parentis* for six hours each day. Only a truly ignorant man could dare to suggest that the Women's Movement of the last century and brave Josephine Butler actually 'put off' the day of women's emancipation. I boiled at that insult to a brave saint! Trust a man to think of women's liberation in terms of men's sexual licence.

Understandably, with so much media coverage of establishment voices, the public discussion for and against parents tended to become standardised to some extent. However the degree of divergence of experience within the teaching profession – who are largely the source of the propaganda to the young – was quite extraordinary. So much seemed to depend on their own subjective opinions, even on matters as complex as the sexual morality of their pupils.

The following angry letter, from a Suffolk teacher and mother of two – pre-adolescent – children, typifies this kind of free-floating subjectivism:

'I have just heard the news that your High Court action has succeeded. How can I convey to you the horror at what you have done? Whilst I have tremendous respect for your strength and determination, your ignorance of what life is like for most people, and your arrogance in assuming that you do know, appals me.

103

As someone who has spent a large part of the last three years working with teenagers as a tutor and counsellor, and whose mother works in a Family Planning Clinic, and who can still well remember the traumas of adolescence, I *know* that breakdown in parental relationships at this time is very widespread. Now you may not like that fact, and you may smugly feel that it will never happen to your relationship with your daughters, but it may well be a lot healthier for their future development if it is. By which I mean that, central to the maturing of any adult is that phase of rejection, rebellion, then hopefully, acceptance of, the parental power and authority which is exercised over all children to greater and lesser degrees. Similarly there is an inevitable process through which parents go as their children begin to demonstrate their need for independence, their sexuality (concomitant with puberty, much as you may dislike the fact), a process which often leads to total communications breakdown. Desperately sad though I find the fact, this breakdown often leads to girls seeking love and approval through sexual relationships. Do you *honestly* believe that any of this can be solved by making it illegal for them to be given confidential contraceptive advice?

In all the hundreds of teenagers I have worked with there have been *three* who have had the sort of relationship with their parents which has allowed them to discuss sexual matters at home. *None* of the others have had that, in fact the vast majority of them have not even been told the facts of life by their parents. I find this desperately sad also, as I expect you do, given the vast array of sexual messages that we are all bombarded with via the media and advertising.

I totally understand and sympathise with the point of principle upon which you launched this campaign, and I would defend your right as an individual parent to enter into a personal contract with your own GP as to the treatment of your own daughters. But to be so irresponsible and arrogant as to believe that you also have the right to dictate as to how other parents' children should be treated disgusts me. You have a naïve and ill informed view of other people's relationships – I suggest you try breaking out of your idyllic little retreat from the world, to see a bit more of how it actually operates. Perhaps you could start a teenage mother and baby unit – God knows we're going to need more after what you've done. I hope that knowledge brings you joy.'

This kind of hard-nosed, humanistic, 'we-don't-live-in-an-ideal-world-so-let's-face-reality,' approach to childhood, contrasts painfully with the concerns of the next writer from Hertfordshire:

'It is only when such individuals as yourself give example and witness to the natural and civilised laws, that a society is given salutory reminders that greed and self-indulgence can so subtly advance and degrade that society through its purely secular and political machinations.

As a Headteacher and father of three I become more and more dismayed and worried how so many teachers and parents seemingly neglect or are painlessly unaware of the vital and sensitive care required for young people between 12 and 16, in view of their tender developments in both body and mind, amid this challenging and changing world. It is therefore even more incredible to me that a State department and medical profession between them can arrange the policy you are rejecting in a so-called "caring" society. You can then imagine how the knowledge of your challenge and belief has heartened so many like myself, who are in agreement with so much that your action implies. God bless your quest.'

With such widely differing attitudes amongst teachers towards their pupils, it is small wonder that compulsory sex instruction is subject to a variety of interpretations – not least by the children at the receiving end! A teacher from Middlesex wrote on this aspect of children's lives:

'I am a teacher and the (High Court) decision

105

yesterday has implications for schools. Sex education in my view is far too narrowly presented and the utilitarian, mechanistic, secularist approach too often taken, robs the debate of the deeper emotional and spiritual features which should underpin proper discussion on these intimate questions.'

Another teacher from London was equally unimpressed with the present methods of imparting the 'facts of life' to schoolchildren:

'As a teacher I have witnessed over the years the slow degrading of youth thanks to the media, ''progressive educational'' theories, especially on sex education etc., etc. Children were still children when I started off, relatively innocent and not sexually aware at all until late teens. How very different today – and often unpleasantly so. I need not expand on what must be obvious to you. I have been especially affronted by the antics of biology teachers and others in their rush to present the facts of life in a grossly mechanical and harmful way – and the extraordinary amoral readiness of adults who ought to know better, whether doctors or so-called advisors, to countenance the dishing out of contraceptives to those below 16. We are not a logical nation, but illogically could scarcely be taken further and to such harmful effect.'

A Hampshire teacher agreed with me to an extent; but took issue with me on the rôle of schools:

'As a teacher and father of two teenage daughters, I am aware of some of your anxieties, although I feel we may also have our disagreements. As a teacher I would not support your claim – according to the press! – that schools encourage promiscuity; as an upper school tutor I suffer some of the pressures from the after effects on my charges – but schools, like yourself, are fighting tremendous external pressures, from society in general, but mainly from parental example and the media. Where I do agree with you is that to make

106

decisions for which the parents must take ultimate responsibility, but where the parents are kept ignorant of any decision making, is thoroughly irresponsible as a system and completely unfair to parents, casting as nought the efforts made during the formative years. For parental involvement in such discussions and all decision making, I support you.

If ultimately there is a case whereby one must recognise that the girl's behaviour is incorrigible despite advice by parents, school and society, then I would not support your cause if your aim were to prohibit contraceptive advice.'

As to that last point, I fail to understand why he did not widen the argument just a wee bit more, to take into account the 'incorrigible behaviour' of the boys concerned. Or are they assumed always to be the victims of the blandishments and seductive powers of over-sexed schoolgirls? Are they blameless? The law says otherwise. If boys had to take the Pill as a palliative against the consequences of the unlawful acts they were committing, then the doctor, teacher, social worker and all else, who helped them on their way, would most certainly be implicated in their actions. As it is, the boys get off scot-free every time.

It's all very well for some teachers to lay the blame on 'parental example and the media' for the bad behaviour in the classroom and behind the cycle shed. But I doubt very much whether, in the nineteen hundreds, when teachers were often dealing with the first generation of children to be given the opportunity to read and write, they blamed these same parents for their children's lack of knowledge. After all, the whole purpose of education, surely, is to give children an opportunity to eat of the fruits of learning, from the branches of those who had fruit in abundance to bestow, namely the teaching profession. In the bad old days, teachers had far greater poverty, ignorance and fear to overcome, while handing on their wisdom.

Yet they *blamed* no one, because they had a vision for society. They believed they were the source of enlightenment to the educationally deprived. Where has that vision gone? It is a poor workman indeed, who not only blames his perfectly new tools, but the manufacturers of them as well.

Once a teacher begins to blame others for the moral shortcomings amongst his pupils, he might as well blame those others for the children's illiteracy, lack of historical knowledge, philistine attitude towards literature, utter ignorance of musical form, or scientific theory etc., etc. – when they finally reach the fifth form. If they have not appreciated any of these things, in all the years they have spent supposedly studying them, then presumably it is because they have either *not* been taught them or been taught badly. You cannot blame the parents or the media for it.

Now since sex education has been in most schools in some form or other, for the best part of twenty years, and has been compulsorily integrated in most State schools for the last ten of them, those children who are displaying symptoms of incorrigible sexual delinquency have either not been taught at all, or, more likely, been taught very badly indeed. I cannot see how the teachers can excuse themselves otherwise.

Schools have taken it upon themselves to be the vehicles for social change and policy. They preach health education and political principles every day in class; condemning smoking, drinking, drug-taking, nuclear warfare, unprotected sex and repressive parents.

If schoolchildren are found to be ignoring much of their advice, and 'doing their own thing' instead, can we fairly assume that the message is either not getting across, or that the advice given by teachers in 'personal development and self-expression' is being taken literally by the young, to the ultimate detriment of the community and themselves?

Can sex and contraceptive instruction ever be taught to children in a moral vacuum and not be even the teeniest, weeniest bit inviting? I very much doubt it; unless it is imparted in a totally po-faced, puritanical manner, fraught with dire warnings of nasty consequences, horrid diseases and primitive taboos.

108

If music was taught to the young, on the principle that they learnt to appreciate the many pleasures of music, without ever hearing a note played, how instruments were handled, without ever being allowed to touch a single one; and with the strict instruction that it was a form of entertainment only to be indulged in when they left school at 16; who would be surprised if a fair number of their more curious pupils disobeyed their mentors and secretly 'had a go'? And why not? After all, if there was no sound moral argument given in favour of abstention, why should they not do so?

Since most parents, apparently, do *not* talk to their children about sex, and most schools *do* and yet we are now witnessing a 'copulation explosion' then the conclusion must be 'let the cap fit where it may'.

A lazy, ignorant or amoral parent can only bring harm to his or her own small handful of children; but a teacher displaying similar qualities, or even being fundamentally hostile to making moral judgements about anything, can influence or deprive hundreds of children during his working life. Just as he can do infinite good, he can also do irreversible harm.

A Southampton social worker showed what good can be done. She also happened to be amongst those who collected signatures for the Public Petition:

'This issue has aroused many people who, believe it or not, did not know that doctors did prescribe the Pill. In my voluntary work (social) among the young and their parents, one can see at first hand the results of the Pill given freely to teenagers! As one girl – not yet 16 – told me it was as though society said go ahead and have sex etc. – you're safe!! After a long discussion with her on the problems of permissiveness and the fact that the Pill does *NOT* protect her from VD (*so* many quite believe it does) she has stopped the Pill and even she wants to sign, but I've told her "she has seen the light" – and has no need to do any more!'

A mother from Lancashire put her finger on the problem in a very short space:

'The prevalent male view of females as sex objects, accepted by so much of society as the norm, is the biggest stumbling block I fear.'

So much a 'norm' has this view become, that a company selling 'condoms' actually displayed huge adverts all over London recently, with the words 'Menswear for Women'. As somebody commented about them: 'White flannels are "menswear for cricket" and a tracksuit is "menswear for jogging".' Thus women are reduced to the level of a de-personalised activity or thing, for the convenience and satisfaction of men.

The views of a seventeen year old girl from Cambridgeshire highlighted difficulties which many a liberated adult chooses to ignore:

'Doctors prescribing the "pill" to underage girls are breaking any relationship of trust between the girl and her mother. It is not the doctor who has to live with the girl in a family, it is just a small part of his daily routine, but the parents have to live with a young girl who is going behind their backs all the time, which probably results in feelings of guilt and, to the parents, unexplained tension in the household.

When I was much younger I remember some girls in my school were given the Pill by their doctors, and at the time my reaction was one of complete shock; although I was too young to form a real opinion because of lack of knowledge on all sides, I was astounded.'

Even in the late Seventies the issue was still largely undebated in the public arena. The experience of a Surrey mother explains the dilemma many parents faced at the time:

'As the mother of a daughter, now 18, I am writing to congratulate you on maintaining your efforts to see that parents are informed when their daughters under 16 are put on the Pill. As daughters get older, the problem disappears and parents tend no longer to concern themselves with the matter, once their own family ceases to be worried. My memories of my own preoccupation with this problem and the blank-wall attitude of my doctor's doctor-wife, to whom I went for advice, remain with me.'

It is widely claimed by some, that because a girl cannot tell her mother that she wants to have sex with a boyfriend, therefore, *ipso facto*, the parental 'relationship' has broken down. What rubbish! It isn't that the girl cannot talk to her mother, but that she *dare* not do so. Neither would any boy wish to tell his dad that he wanted cash to buy cigarettes or to go into a pub or to buy condoms for use with his underage girlfriend. What normal children ever voluntarily tell their parents that they intend doing something wrong? So the girls go to a doctor and forbid him to 'grass' on them to anyone, and hide their three months' supply of drugs under their mattress.

On the word of a child, the parent is cast as the authoritarian villain, whilst the family-planner soaks up all the kudos for being a kindly, caring counsellor.

A father of two children wrote from Kent and posed a question to doctors:

'An argument I have not yet heard, or have possibly missed in defence of parental care is: "How can a doctor or any other person understand a young person's state of mind or mental make-up after two or three short interviews, and at the end of the day with hand on heart, truthfully and honestly say 'I was correct'. Surely parents are more aware of their children and know infinitely better than all the "do gooders" their every turn and thought that their own youngsters are likely to make and think?'

My comment on one part of that letter, is that the writer is badly overestimating the time a doctor allots to a child he intends giving the Pill. In some clinics, the girl can be in and out within ten minutes during her lunch break, and not too many awkward questions asked in the time. The

Family Planning Association proudly boasts, that no girl leaves their clinics 'unprotected' after their *FIRST* visit
. . . .

If family relationships are truly bad, something needs to be done at once, for the sake of the children. The following letter from Kent explains what so often happens, when nothing is done at all, until much too late:

'For some years my work was in various penal establishments for young and old, male and female; and it became increasingly apparent that attacks on family life brings greater instability in society. In my mind those who advocate ready availability of contraception for youngsters are deliberately seeking to wreck families – to increase the growth of sexual problems and to destroy all Christian principles.'

Since this chapter is concerned with the common experience of people, it may be useful at this point to look at some of the common assumptions of some of them also.

One of the people who involved themselves with collecting signatures for the Public Petition, did his own door-to-door survey of public opinion on this issue. He said it was very interesting. He spoke to about 70 people, mostly women, and found that they were 7 – 1 in favour of parents being told about contraceptives given to their daughters.

Reasons for disagreement varied. Some believed that there were instances when it was better the parents should *not* be told. Some mothers even said they would not mind if they themselves were not told!

There was apparently much confusion as to what 'at risk' meant. Prevalent was the view that girls were going to have sex anyway, even if they didn't want their parents told.

Cogent argument, statistics and quotations left these women unconvinced; they held to the belief that *every* argument carried its own statistics.

There was also great faith in doctors, that they would do the right thing by a girl, including giving her decent, paternal advice, and trying to dissuade her from deceiving her parents where possible. In an ideal world, where all medics were potential, if not actual, saints, this might be possible and true.

The reality is somewhat more prosaic. Country practices, often as not, know the ins and outs of everyone's lives. It would be extremely difficult to keep secrets from anyone for long. But in towns and cities, where large multiple practices flourish, a girl can easily visit a GP not even her own, and be fairly sure he won't suddenly turn up in her home on a flying visit. Clinics, of course, hardly practice home visiting at all, and have no close relationship with individual families.

Two former family planning nurses wrote separately of their experiences. The first from Cheshire:

'I was a founder and Chairman of a local FPA clinic in the 1950s but eventually resigned after a fight against the gradual slide, to what we considered to be their slide, to supporting the modern outlook on sexual permissiveness.

I was always sad to hear that all doctors, except RCs, took the attitude that moral issues were none of their business.

It is incredible and disgraceful that a potentially dangerous drug like the Pill can be prescribed to a young girl without the parents' knowledge, when the parents are responsible for their child's welfare till the age of consent. In fact I do not think that *any* drugs should be prescribed to under 16s without the parents' knowledge.'

Again, in the second letter from Gloucestershire, it seems to be the involvement of the NHS that causes all the problems:

'I worked for the Family Planning Clinic in a voluntary position, when it was run as a charity, just to provide a good service for Family Planning only. The NHS took over and from then on I became utterly disillusioned and left when I could no longer bear to see what was going on.'

Another nurse wrote from Oxfordshire:

'I must say the whole thing is just nonsense when one really comes to think of it as a whole; one minute parents are blamed for the wrongs their children get up to, or into, then they (whoever they are) refuse to co-operate with parents in very grave matters, moral, medical and psychological; poor little girls and all youngsters, are hardly formed mentally or physically and certainly not spiritually, it really makes one wonder what the medical profession is coming to? In my days of training, all parents had to be consulted before the smallest treatments were carried out; in fact parents were encouraged to sit with the infants and all young children for as long as they could and meals were provided, also accommodation if they so wished, and most certainly *ALL* parents had to sign forms for their children's treatments, or "ops". Also all young adults, teenagers etc., had to have an escort, and a chaperone when visiting a doctor of any kind.'

A school dental nurse from Devon also explained the position regarding 'consent to treatment':

'The School Dental Service has the right in law to inspect every child attending State aided schools, the parents being notified of our visit and invited to attend for consultation if they desire. Where a child is found to require dental treatment, and where we think it is not currently receiving treatment, we send the parents a form pointing out that treatment is available under the GDS or School Dental Service; if the parent wishes us to treat, they sign the black slip at the bottom of the form, and if they elected to go for the GDS, they sign the red part of the form. At no time do we treat a child without the requisite "permission form" being signed by the parent. Further, at no time would we give a general anaesthetic without a "responsible adult" being present to take the child home (not a 16 year old brother or sister) as our legal responsibility only ends when the patient is handed over to a responsible adult;

otherwise if the patient was dazed and fell under a bus on the way home we would be legally responsible. As you may well imagine, in 29 years working in a rural area we built up a tremendous *rapport* with the parents and children and were constantly approached for help and discussion in the towns and villages in our area, and always complied, but always "with permission".'

Early in 1985 an internal ballot was taken by School Nurses, as to their own views on schoolgirls and the Pill, and whether or not they thought that parents ought to be asked first.

Having met a few of these nurses over the years, with so many of my children passing through their hands (literally, in the case of 'Nitty Norahs'!), I have always found them to be the sweetest, kindest and most honest of women. Their straightforward but tactful approach seemed always to be geared to helping us mothers in every way possible. They somehow managed to enhance our rôle, making us feel vitally necessary in our children's lives. I never minded being corrected or advised by them. Their concern was always genuine, and founded on good commonsense.

So I was not really surprised that their ballot revealed that most of them were very much in favour of parental involvement in their daughters' sexual development.

However, to be fair to them, they did see both sides of the problem, as one such nurse and mother from Warwickshire so clearly explained:

'I'm afraid the Law is being, not for the first time, the proverbial "ass", and I agree with you that if parents are to retain responsibility for their children in other aspects, up to the age of 16 (and in some aspects to the age of 18) we must have responsibility for the tremendously important issue of sexual activity, even if it means having to accept a doctor's advice that our sexually precocious daughters ought to be protected by contraception. To do even this we must *KNOW*.

As a nurse employed recently in the school nursing service at secondary school level, I know that the age of

16 is the great divide as far as medical matters go, and if parents have to give consent for medical examinations, vaccinations, dental treatment, and suchlike, I cannot see that we can be legally deprived of mere knowledge of contraceptive provision, for girls below that age.

One has to accept that for too many children today, caring parents do not exist, they may be feckless, inadequate, or simply not there – the struggle to merely exist means that single parents may well not have the energy or time to cope with wayward teenagers, and this goes for boys in the matter of vandalism, as well as the girls in the matter of sexual promiscuity – there is no parent to care or control – what can we say when such girls need advice and protection – should they be put ''in care'' or is it likely that as prison makes criminals, community ''homes'' make prostitutes? One has to admit that these are very difficult problems, and I despair of a solution. Does one have to accept that, like the poor, promiscuity will be always with us, or can one hope for a swing to morality, so that all girls will not be pushed into activities once only indulged in by the ''bad'' ones? I'm afraid that with the invention of the contraceptive pill, it is an irreversible situation. The girls can now behave as boys always have, and with no more rebuke than a sigh or a shrug! But as a caring parent, I still should *know*.'

It *cannot* be 'irreversible', no society could sustain such a breakdown in social order without Government itself collapsing. If one in three marriages are breaking down *today*, leaving single parents to cope alone and 100,000 children in 'care', we must recall that these parents are the product of the Sixties, when promiscuity was still only relatively rare amongst very young teenagers, and only indulged in widely among much older girls. Promiscuity is a training in instability, lack of commitment and a fear of life. It robs women of their instinctive moral strength to withstand the hard knocks that marriage, children, unemployment or illness may bring them. They become deeply uncertain of their own individual worth as people,

116

when constant rejection and infidelity become a pattern of life from early on. Neither is a wayward and selfish youth likely to make the best of fathers or the most constant of husbands.

So what future has any community, when promiscuity and fecklessness begins in *secondary* schools? No government can withstand the financial burden of running a society, where so many families or individuals are in need of State aid; and where the projected, earning and tax paying workforce is reduced to 2 adults for every old age pensioner, as is predicted by the year 2025

The stability of the family – of parents and children together – is crucial to the very existence of the State itself.

But back to reality! A former Assistant Matron in a Church of England Moral Welfare Home gave some ideas as to why young girls became involved in sexuality, thirty years ago:

'I came to the following conclusions why girls indulge in pre-marital sexual activity: (1) Boredom: the only interest for most of the girls were boys, dances, cinema and Radio Luxemburg. (2) Loneliness and the need for love; disinterested parents; lack of self-esteem. Peer pressure is added to this now. (3). A craving for motherhood. Girls whose babies were adopted would sometimes need to repeat the process several times. Abortion probably has a similar result. Contraception does nothing to fulfil this need!'

She is probably very right on that last point. Yet there is a sad correlation between the widespread use of contraception and a vastly increased uptake in the use of licenced abortion, all over the world. Even a doctor working in the Edinburgh 'Brooks' abortion agency had to admit this fact, in an article in *The Scotsman*. She stated that, contrary to what you might expect, an increase in contraceptive use means a rise in the numbers of abortions to the users. Not so much because contraceptive measures, such as the low dose hormone pill, are notoriously risky when used by unreliable and unstable

117

teenagers (which they are), but chiefly because a contraceptive mentality has been created, which disassociates the sexual act from its natural life-giving potential. Where once a girl who risked intercourse, unprotected by drugs or devices, became pregnant, and would have accepted such an outcome fatalistically and carried on to have the child, now such an occurrence is regarded as totally unacceptable and untoward; almost as if nature had ratted on them and given them a nasty disease.

Doctors, sometimes inadvertently and sometimes deliberately, have fostered and encouraged this idea amongst women, and have thereby treated 'contraceptive failure' as a legitimate ground for an abortion.

If saying 'no' was never very easy for some schoolgirls, even in the mid '50s when around 500 of them became pregnant, by the 1980s the widespread teaching and distribution of contraceptives has done little to help them along, with 8,500 of them falling foul of nature's fertile whims and five thousand of those conceptions ending up in hospital incinerators.

Yet despite all the evidence that contraception has done little or nothing to improve marital relationships, the care of 'planned' children, or the health and security of teenagers, some men still seem to think that the solution to current social dilemmas lies in a packet of hormone drugs. A young social worker from Wales reiterates the old, old story:

'The function of contraception is prevention of *unwanted* babies. I know there are agencies for adoption and that ''unplanned' children do not equate with unloved children – this latter from personal experience. Also, though, I know of the unhappiness, bitterness, damage that is suffered by or inflicted by unwanted, unloved young people – again through personal experience of working with people – under sixteen years of age – in care. I would go so far as to say that in my experience, which I believe to be typical – 95% of all young people in care are the consequence of not having stable, loving parents who *want* them.

You and I are lucky. I hope our children will be. However, your action will cause more sadness, unhappiness and despair to enter the world through unwanted teenage pregnancies and abortions – because young people will not stop experimenting with or indulging in sexual intercourse because of the law or a defined (16 years) birthday. It is those who are most at risk, i.e. those who cannot talk to their parent(s) who are the ones you have thrust beyond the help and advice of caring, compassionate people concerned with family planning.'

To that I would counter, that young people will not stop 'experimenting with or indulging in sexual intercourse', whilst young men are *not* taught to abstain until married or to regard women and girls as so much easy prey, regardless of the hurt and harm they do them and the community in which they live.

It would also help young people to withstand the pressures put upon them, to conform to this kind of delinquent behaviour, if those magazines directed specifically at the young, such as *O Boy*, *My Guy*, *Just 17* and all the rest, didn't harp on about it so much or make sex the be-all and end-all of a girl's thought processes. It might be a good moneyspinner for the wealthy owners of these little propaganda broadsheets, but for my money they represent the truly 'unacceptable face of Capitalism'.

As can be seen, opinions vary enormously, and are never very hard to find. Put another way, by a Suffolk father of five:

'Everyone, without exception has a point of view. There would be no spoilt votes in this ballot!'

Seven: 'Hard Cases'

Through the whole of this long drawn-out, emotion-charged debate, the 'hard case' has been made a central issue. It was inevitable that both sides of the argument would want to submit evidence of how well or ill the DHSS policy was working, how the intervention of law into human affairs could create either chaos or care.

Every radio, television or newspaper article which attempted to 'investigate' the matter, drew upon the experience of doctors, sex-counsellors, gynaecologists and children, and paraded them before us, replete with all their grizzly tales of abortions, near deaths, incestuous pregnancies and suicides; maniacal fathers and feckless mothers; infections, cancers, infertility; the imposition of religious morality upon private sexual freedoms, and all the rest . . . .

Yet in all such determined attempts by producers and participants to fight their own particular corner, I have yet to see, hear or read of any one of them allowing even the tiniest space to those who are at the heart of this particular debate. No – I don't mean the girls or boys themselves, for plenty of them have been given an abundance of air time and newspaper columns to state their views.

I'm talking about the *parents*. Those who have been deceived by doctors and have found out too late what has been done. You'll never see them on your telly screen, or hear them complain on a 'File on Four' radio documentary. They don't appear in newspapers and they won't speak to reporters.

I know from personal experience that producers often want them to come forward. Naturally they won't, and who would blame them? Haven't they been hurt and shamed enough, by being regarded by a doctor or social worker or judge as a 'bad' parent, 'uncaring' or 'out of touch'?

Would anyone but the most steely-hearted parent, want to parade themselves, their failures, their families, before an audience of hostile and fault-finding people? I would think not. Indeed I would *hope* not. Any parent prepared to scandalise their children in such a public and selfish manner would be uncaring in the extreme.

No, you won't find a deceived parent anywhere, prepared to go to such horrendous lengths to prove a point. So their voice has gone unheard.

But I have heard them; they have written to me. Not many of them; but enough to give anyone a genuine insight into that 'other side' of the hard case story.

Some of them were obviously too distressed to give me any specific details. They just wrote as did this mother from Cambridgeshire:

> 'I know from experience that children need supervision when taking any course of drugs, so that side effects can be monitored, yet the DHSS sees fit to dish out, via family doctors, "the pill", a potent drug, thereby lowering parental authority, creating deceit within the family and flouting the law as it stands.
>
> The problem has affected my family personally and has diminished my confidence in the doctor concerned. Fortunately my daughter and I have been able to talk about it and this has helped.

A mother from Sussex wrote about a local day school, where pupils received an active Christian education. She wished her daughter had gone there, adding:

> ' . . . the doctor here must have persuaded her to go "on the pill" between 16 – 17. I couldn't get him because she was over age, but I have not forgiven him or forgotten. I was a widow at the time and it nearly drove me mad, worrying about it. She went through a rebellious stage, but would not have been so daring, if she had not had the opportunity, I'm sure.'

Whilst telling me of their own experience, mothers usually have something to say about the wider issues, as did this one from Edinburgh:

'I admire you deeply for having the courage to stand up and speak out against the whole philosophy of the Family Planning Association. I can see that non-Roman Catholic wives, who have all the children they want, can need the expertise of the FPA, but I do feel the effect of their work has been to bring about a great change in customs regarding marriage and sex.

I have three daughters of my own, all older, ranging from 18 to 22. My advice about no sex outside of marriage did not stand up for all of them, in the face of social pressures at University, and even at school. One of them, the pressure of opinion at a mixed school sent her, after her 16th birthday, to the nearby FPA clinic, and they put her on the Pill, with very few questions asked or warnings given. Their main objective is to avoid unwanted pregnancies, and thereby to remove a cause of baby-battering.

We went through a very difficult period of unhappiness on both sides. The daughter in question entered far too soon into relationships with boys, and had one real rejection. I think now she is beginning to see the dangers of it all, and is prepared to wait for someone more faithful to come along one day. However, I feel she has had a bad experience which should not have happened. Now, at 18, she has taken herself off the pill.

Any talk of lowering the age of consent to 12 or giving pills to the under 16s only encourages the boys to put pressure on girls. Another point which occurs to me is this: how would the boys react if *they* were expected to take pills which might lead to side effects such as embolism, infertility and some of the other predicaments which face long-term users of the Pill? Obviously it is all a very emotive subject, but I am so glad you have taken up the cudgel.'

In 1983, Clement Freud passed a letter on to me from a Southampton mother, who wrote with great clarity on the parent/child relationship and the family.

'She' (that's me) 'is speaking for very many anxious

mothers. I am gravely concerned that our legal system can allow such a significant undermining of the principles of parenthood and the protection of children. What the present judgement implies is that the only protection our under-sixteens need from sexual activity is the protection against conception. This ridiculous notion flies in the face of all that ordinary people know about children under sixteen, about present sexual pressures and about the sometimes devastating effect of sexual involvement in early adolescence. We are not protecting children, but making them increasingly vulnerable, if we remove the parents from their rôle of "guardians" as regards this issue. I understand that a Ward of Court would not be allowed contraception without the Court's permission – are we moving towards a situation where the state and the Courts usurp traditional parental rights as regards the appropriate terms of care and protection of children? Sociologists continually stress the value and importance of family, for both individual and social benefit, but we are seeing a progressive attack on family relationships, evidenced by the present right of a doctor to keep secret from a mother issues which would surely affect the family: the very change of responsibility to the doctor lessens the influence of the mother's rôle in preparing her daughter for adulthood.

I am now a mother of three. However, I was once a pre-sixteen involved in sexual activity (without parental knowledge for some time) and I do know what a terrible trap it can be. The possibility of easy contraception would have made me even more vulnerable to pressure for more sexual involvement. It was a great relief (though traumatic) when my parents eventually found out and I found great strength in their care.

The urgency of this short London letter speaks volumes:

'We support you with praise for your energy and true purpose over the rôle and rights of parenthood. I was shocked when I learnt that our 14 year old stepdaughter had been put on the Pill without our knowledge. I am most anxious that my own two daughters are protected from any sexual experience until they are at least seventeen or more. But it is a scandal to think that a doctor can give them the Pill, under age. My eleven year old is very unaware of the dangers, temptations and emotions that lie in wait for her as a teenager.'

Have you noticed how many 'RIGHTS' there are in the world these days? Everybody has them: children, parents, doctors, the State. Like barrack-room lawyers, each one urging his case upon the other.

So let's look at each one separately, and give at least a brief summary of their Rights:

Children have Rights: lots of them. A right to be housed, clothed, fed, watered; medicated, educated and protected from criminal harm – all these and many more Rights up to the age of 18 years. What is more, they don't even have to provide them for themselves, but can, and do, demand them of others: their parents, doctors, teachers etc. They have duties too: to obey the Law and the wise advice of their parents as legal guardians.

Parents have Rights: A few of them. To marry, conceive children and bring them up as best they can. These are natural, freestanding, self-evident Rights. What they choose is best for their children, is a matter for their judgement, within the normal confines of the Law, and with the wise advice of others, if needs be. They have a Right to State Aid in certain circumstances, when requested. Their duties are both moral and legal: morally they are bound to fulfil those obligations which natural parenthood invites; whilst the Law ensures that they do not backslide on them, to such an extent that their children are placed in dire moral or physical harm, or disadvantaged beyond immediate repair.

Doctors have Rights: Again a few of them. To practice their art with integrity, according to their good conscience, and within the confines of the Law, and the traditional ethical code of their profession. A doctor's

124

duty is to "do no harm" to his patients, or co-operate
in any way with others who might wish him to do so.

The State, via its Civil Servants and Agencies, has a duty
to provide such services as Parliament has given it leave;
and a right to demand payment from the public for the
provision of them.

But what happens if the State-run Civil Service
demands from one of its paid Agents, i.e. doctors, that
they perform duties which conflict with those of parents,
to the detriment of their children? That is what you call a
monumental *conflict* of interests!

A Surrey mother revealed what happened in her own
family's case:

'My youngest daughter is now 16 years old, but when
she was fourteen and a half, about six months after her
periods began, she came out in a rash which was
eventually diagnosed as Nervous Scoreocis. There
appeared no reason for this complaint but she did have
many minor ailments in the months that followed,
including headaches, self-imposed starvation and
finally a very serious case of anaemia. All this time she
was under the doctor for an infection of the womb and
vagina. Because her periods were very irregular and
heavy, the doctor put her on the Pill, with my
permission, to regulate them. Then she had to visit a
gynaecologist and have an internal examination. What
they discovered from this was never disclosed to me,
even though I asked to speak to the gynaecologist
concerned. By this time she was fifteen. It was decided
to keep her on the Pill for a further six months.
Through another incident which occurred with another
member of the family, I was told that my 15 year old
daughter was having a sexual relationship with a
married man. After a lot of questioning of my daughter
I discovered that this man had got her drunk one night,
while baby-sitting for friends, and raped her, then
continued the relationship until I discovered it was
going on, six months after she was examined by the
gynaecologist. She and I suffered 12 months of anguish

125

and uncertainty and yet this could have been curtailed if the doctors etc., had told me about her condition. She is still, at the age of sixteen and a quarter suffering from an infection she contracted from this man. If she had had scarlet fever or diptheria I would have been told, so why not about this? I think it is all wrong that parents be kept in the dark about these things. If we are expected to be responsible for them by Law until they are 18, then we are entitled to know all the facts. If I had let her sleep with this man or any others, in my house, I could have been accused of encouraging sex with a girl under age. But because the Department of Health say so, *they* are not committing a crime.

The prosecution of this man is still in the balance so I don't want my name printed, but I support your campaign wholeheartedly.'

It was a terrible story, but it does go to show that for every 'hard case' story that you may hear from a child – or family planning doctor – there is *ALWAYS* the other side to be understood and given sympathy.

Time and again we hear from the DHSS – even their Appeal to the House of Lords is redolent with it – that their policy was meant for the 'exceptional case' where parents had completely abandoned their responsibilities and left their children to fend for themselves. But if this isn't a downright dishonesty, then it surely amounts to culpable stupidity. For how can any clinic doctor possibly know, for certain, that such a situation exists, unless and until they have taken every possible opportunity to find out, either themselves, or with the assistance of others?

If a child was to present to a doctor symptoms of physical abuse or neglect, he would not hesitate to take immediate action to have the family circumstances carefully investigated. The very fact that a child is seeking contraceptive or abortion advice from him, in secret, should be sufficient evidence that something was wrong at home or with the girl herself. Alarm bells should be ringing in his head! Is it incest? Is it an older man, married or with paedophile tendencies? Has she become a prostitute? Will she catch an infection of her internal organs that will bring endless 'gyny' problems later on?

For doctors simply to prescribe several months' supply of a hormone drug (which is then picked up by the girl at the local chemist shop on the way to school), whilst washing their hands of all the dangers and complications that will follow, is tantamount to gross medical neglect.

Such behaviour by a once-trusted and honourable profession, has done little to enhance the rôle of the doctor in the eyes of the community. It has, equally, done great and widespread harm to the nature and rôle of parenthood, in the eyes of their adolescent daughters.

The following personal account, from a Birmingham mother, describes how this can happen:

'My youngest daughter was prescribed the Pill when she was aged about fourteen because of irregularity with her periods. I was angry because the doctor did not consult me and I was totally against the idea because I was concerned about the long term effects, and was not inclined to consider that the Pill was the only possible remedy. However, the doctor had convinced my daughter and she took the Pill as prescribed. With hindsight she could have been in considerable danger – her grandmother and more recently her father suffered severe strokes, and in the past I have suffered thrombosed veins; as we now know, these are hereditary factors which, combined with the Pill, can put the user in jeopardy. She is now twenty two and has been married for just over two years; she discontinued using the Pill as both she and her husband are anxious to start a family and although it is early days yet, she is bitterly disappointed that, so far, they have not succeeded; she is now worried that the use of the Pill during her years of puberty may have had an adverse effect in this direction – time will tell.'

Have you ever noticed those posters in doctors' waiting rooms, warning parents not to send their children under 16 along to surgery for inoculations, unaccompanied by an adult? Perhaps it would be a wiser precaution if that poster advice was extended, to cover *all* consultations of whatever nature.

127

Another mother, from Surrey, wrote about her observations on a family close to her:

> 'I know of a number of girls (admittedly over 16) and especially of one who is very close to me, who regret that their parents condoned their decision to go on the Pill – one girl is extremely bitter towards her mother and blames her for her emotional problems to a large degree.
>
> How *dare* outsiders take over the rights of parents to tell children facts which are delicate in themselves and should be spoken of in *LOVE*?'

Poor parents! If they stand out against the Pill, the medical profession calls them irresponsible; and if they agree to it, their children call them foolish . . . . What unutterable confusion!

The following letter from a stepmother in Glamorgan graphically describes what happened when the child from a 'bad' family background was put on the Pill, supposedly to 'protect' her from further neglect.

> 'My stepdaughter has been on the Pill since she was 13, she had no guidance from her mother with whom she was living. What girl, after experiencing relationships with boys, can concentrate on her studies? She stayed on in school until she was 18 and left without any qualifications. She lives in a squat and has already experienced "gyny" problems and has laser treatment to kill cancerous cells. All this, what a waste of a young girl's potential.'

Often, the anger was against the drug itself, and not any sexual relationships associated with it. A Middlesex mother wrote about her own daughter:

> 'In 1975 a chance remark from a doctor's receptionist revealed that my 16 year old daughter had been prescribed the birth pill.
>
> Disconcerting as I found this fact, having an aversion to the indiscriminate use of drugs of any kind, I was

much more concerned by the secrecy surrounding the matter and by the receptionist's anxiety about her mistake of accidentally informing a parent that her 16 year old daughter was on the Pill.

Having noticed a certain irritability and complaints of various pains in legs and body by my daughter, over the past few weeks, I had been rather concerned about the possible cause as she has always been in very good health. I feel it would have been helpful if I had known the situation. My daughter's reticence about the matter was due, not to a lack of communication between us, but to my mistrust of drugs in general.

My objection to current practice is based not upon moral issues, which in this case concerns a steady relationship, but to information given to teenagers that the Pill is the only suitable method of contraception. Having seen the undesirable consequences of this method and having for years taken pains to provide a diet as free from harmful additives as possible for my family, I am naturally concerned regarding any threat to their good health.

On the matter of principle, I think it is wrong for a doctor to deliberately hide such information as the prescribing of a specific drug, from the parents of any young person who is in their care, unless there is some possibility that the parents' view will harm the child.

As certain side effects may result from the Pill, it might help the parents to deal patiently with these, if they are aware of the possible cause. For instance, several of my friends have noticed that the Pill made them very bad tempered and this could have an unhappy effect on family life.'

Whilst I sympathise with that mother in many ways – (and I'm sure others would do the same, even more than I) – I cannot help feeling that if your only concern is with the physical health of your children, and you ignore their moral and spiritual dimensions, you have failed to some extent, to care for the *whole* person.

Clearly her doctor thought so too. Only his solution to

the situation was to introduce his *own* moral priorities, in place of the mother's lack of them.

She herself even suggested that this was OK, when she said 'unless there is some possibility that the parents' view will harm the child'. Once you have conceded that another person *can* make judgements about the parent, and can then *act* upon them, you have effectively lost the argument against your own rights.

As to a 16 year old having a 'steady relationship', that seems to me to be meaningless jargon. Nowadays, even one in three *marriages* aren't stable any more! Some parents – nay, many *people* – seem to think that going out with a boy for six months constitutes a 'steady relationship'. Let them make such a claim, after they have stood the trials of 30 years' marriage; then I might believe them!

Whether or not it is as a result of following the DHSS policy for so many years, or just because an individual doctor has an unsympathetic 'bedside' manner anyway, but it does seem to be the case that *some* doctors, at least, are not just indifferent about parents' worries, but are actively hostile to them, over this underage pill prescribing.

Two mothers wrote of their separate experiences in this respect. The first was from South Wales:

'I have two daughters, aged 16 and 7 years and a son of 14 years. I am happily married and have very definite views in respect of children being given the Pill at such an early age and without parents' knowledge. I was pretty upset when I took my elder daughter to the doctor recently with pre-exam nerves and tummy-aches just to make sure she wasn't physically affected. When the doctor examined her in an adjacent room, she questioned her as to whether she had a boyfriend and was there any need for contraception – as she could prescribe it and so on. My daughter of course is 16 years old and more mature than an 11 year old – even so, she has a most unstable and immature relationship with her boyfriend. I feel quite sure that had she been given the Pill she would have had

FRIDAY

11

MARCH

The LORD thy God blesseth thee, as he promised thee.

Deuteronomy 15. 6

O fill me Lord yet more and more,
So that my heart e'en here below,
From Thy love's rich and boundless
    store,
Be satisfied and overflow.
Full with the blessing Thou hast
    given,
The foretaste now of what makes
    heaven.

intercourse, however, and then followed suit with the next boy and the next. Thus putting herself at risk of catching sexually transmitted disease, and the possible side effects of taking the Pill so early in life.

So, to hear that doctors intend giving contraception to children – knowing they are *under age* for legal intercourse – without contacting the parents simply makes me appalled. It is increasingly difficult to monitor one's children's activities and teach them moral values and I feel this ruling can only adversely affect parental control.'

The second mother, whose address was not given, related a similar experience:

'I have three children, and when my youngest daughter was seventeen she had problems which, as a State Registered Nurse, I decided was due to pre-menstrual stress plus examination anxiety. As matters got worse and she was getting more and more aggressive towards myself and her older sister, I sought medical advice, explaining as much as I could to the doctor and asking if he would see her. I also mentioned that she had befriended a young French student who had come to the school for a year, and that I had discussed their relationship as they both wanted nothing to interfere with their promising academic careers. My daughter did go to see the doctor at the appointed time, but he was over an hour late, and although he had told me he would give her a sympathetic hearing and possible examination, she was out in less than two minutes, he having said to her (a) not to tell me what he had said to her, and (b) there was nothing wrong with her that getting away from me and doing what she liked with her own life and with the boyfriend wouldn't cure, and to stick it out until she got away from home to university.

My daughter came home, announcing her disgust and saying she would never, ever, go to see him again, and said he had the impression we were always quarrelling. Half undecided whether or not to study

131

medicine or law, she then said there was no way she would ever now do medicine, and there was no way she was being put on the Pill.

I had to seek alternative treatment for her pre-menstrual stress and am happy to say she is fine now. But the doctor's attitude horrified me and also the knowledge that he is a magistrate. However, I do run the local youth club and often ponder over what he may have prescribed for other young girls.

I should have been very distressed if I had thought my underaged daughter had been prescribed the Pill, but what really bothers me is why isn't anything ever said about the boys? Why are they not discouraged from too young sexual activity, why can't they be told of the dangers of too early sexual activity and the dangers of drugs and internal appliances, AIDS, early cancer and sexually transmitted diseases?'

I have blamed school teachers for the crucial part they have played in encouraging the young to experiment with sex, and how so many of them have unwittingly turned children from fumbling amateurs into wayward professionals. Was I looking for a convenient scapegoat, or do other people feel that schools have ceased to play a significant rôle in civilising society and have simply become a breeding ground for tribal peer groups to flourish? Has the classroom become no longer the antidote to feckless families, but the creator of new ones for the future?

A London mother wrote, 'I write in horror at the moral dangers children face in schools.' She went on to explain:

'A grandmother that I know arrived at my house in tears, because her daughter had just discovered that her two girls, very attractive and normal girls, and completely underage, had been having the Pill for some time, just doled out without their parents' knowledge. There has been terrible unhappiness with unsuitable boyfriends ever since. If you teach a subject – sex – prematurely, you intend your victims to practice the same. It struck me that one was sending the children into a nightmare, and they would be much better off at home.

The only way that one can deal with the cruel and lax attitude towards the welfare of girl children, is that anyone having sex with them goes to borstal or prison, and then there is no argument. The one aspect of the Pill that no one dare mention is the incredible harm the Pill does to the taker. One comes across so many horror stories put down to the Pill and can see the unhappy change in the girl who takes it. These are our loved children that we are abusing.'

Another mother wrote in 1983, to explain how long this trouble had been going on. She left no address, for understandable reasons:

'I am writing to you because it might be of interest to hear of my own experience as long as 13 years ago.

We lived in Hastings then and my daughter was a pupil at the High School. One day when she was 13 years of age, she came home telling me of a lady from the Health Authority who had come to the school, with a case full of samples of contraception, explained them to the children, at the same time mentioning a clinic the children could go to in the evenings and did not have to tell their parents about it. I must point out that no parents were consulted or contacted prior to this lady's visit.

Like you I was furious. We had at that time an RC priest on the Board of Governors as well as an Anglo Catholic one. I made the strongest representations in writing, and verbally, and was simply told there was nothing that could be done. I mean by that, I approached both these priests. Needless to say, a lot of girls went to that clinic. That was 13 years ago. Yet this problem was never ever discussed or brought into the open until you started stamping your feet. Why? It is obvious that the clergy must be aware of it.

I am a lucky woman. My daughter went to her wedding 10 years after the event, in a white dress she was entitled to wear with pride. But it shows that what you are fighting now is in fact not a new problem and you might have to dig much deeper than you think. Very recently there has been much controversy about a similar clinic just started here, where the doctors do not even ask the children their age. But, as ever, the ''baddies'' have won.'

When are we parents supposed to stop caring about our children? At sixteen? – eighteen? The law doesn't reflect love, only legal obligations. For most parents the worry and heartache, pride and joy, goes on for years after such dates.

More than once a parent has written to me about their daughter's behaviour, and *APOLOGISED* because they were over sixteen, and felt they shouldn't be worried about them any more. But 17 and 18 year old girls can be just as immature as a fourteen year old. Some doctors simply won't deal with anyone under eighteen, without their parents knowing, or being present, just because they know that the young person will need adult advice as well as *his* treatment. Their consent to the treatment may very well be 'legally' valid; but their ability to understand the full implications of what they are undertaking is what counts in the end.

For example: how many schoolchildren could tell you what ailments their parents or grandparents may or may not have suffered? Precious few! How many could tell a clinic doctor exactly which illnesses or immunisations they had had, and when precisely? How many girls are therefore being prescribed this hormone drug – with its list of contra-indications as long as your arm – without any proper medical history being taken? When we hear the word 'trust' being bandied about in medical circles, and we know they are talking about children on the Pill, do they really only mean that the *girl* trusts the doctor won't tell her parents, and *he* trusts the girl won't tell them either; and the doctor and the DHSS together trust that no one will complain, while the parents are left to pick up the pieces and take the blame for the whole affair as usual?

It sometimes seems like that.

In the February of 1985, a couple wrote from the West

Country about the tragic results to their own much loved daughter:

'Our 19 year old daughter died after an appendix operation on the 4th January due to a pulmonary embolism, and we were devastated to discover that she had been taking the contraceptive pill for the past six months. Although at the inquest last week cause of death was certified as pulmonary embolism, deep vein thrombosis in the leg and appendicectomy, the doctor who carried out the *post mortem* did say that the Pill could have been a contributory factor in her death. Although we cannot prove it, we will always wonder if she would still be alive today if she had not taken the Pill.

She had had a boyfriend for the past nine months, but as we have always had an open and trusting relationship and she was fully aware of the dangers of pre-marital sex etc., we never for a moment suspected they were having a sexual relationship.

We understand that she obtained the Pill through a Family Planning Clinic, but as this was not through her own family doctor (when it might have been prescribed for period pain) we can only presume it was for contraceptive purposes. We did try to arrange an appointment to see the person who prescribed it, but as the Coroner had asked for her records and was pursuing the matter we left it, thinking we would hear a report at the inquest. However, Family Planning were not represented nor was there a report.

The doctor from the hospital where our daughter had her operation was asked by the Coroner if he was aware that she was on the Pill when admitted into hospital, and he said he was, but that she was taken off whilst there. However, as she was admitted at approximately 6 pm on the 31st December and operated on at 1 am 1st January, even if it was stopped on her admittance the effects would still be in the system. Also, her sister said she was not taken off the Pill whilst in hospital. Unfortunately, we cannot prove this nor would it have had any bearing.

However, we would like to know what precautions Family Planning Clinics take when prescribing the Pill, whether to teenagers or otherwise. As it is well known to cause thrombosis and we already have a history of same on both sides of the family, would this have been checked with our daughter first? Secondly, are patients warned of the dangers and side effects beforehand?

We do not agree with these clinics giving contraceptives to teenagers at all and particularly as they are free of charge. The anomaly is that, on the one hand, we have Norman Fowler stopping free prescriptions of essential drugs to elderly patients, who probably have paid for them over and over again through the National Insurance contributions, paid during their lifetime. On the other hand we have these clinics giving free contraception to unmarried people, and in fact encouraging them to have pre-marital sex at the nation's expense, when the majority could well afford to pay for their own, as is the case of my daughter. Surely, it would be more of a deterrent if they had to pay heavily out of their own pockets?

It will probably be argued that it is far better to use contraceptives than to have unwanted pregnancies; but even though there is all this free advice and issuing of same, it has not stopped the pregnancies. Also the question of sexually transmitted diseases cannot be ignored.'

Once again, I ask – is this an isolated case? In May of this year, a young 17 year old London girl died from taking the Pill. She had been on it since she was fifteen, and death was caused by a cerebral thrombosis. It made a largish splash in the national press and I was reported in some papers as saying:

'It would be considered a national outrage if a 15 year old girl was given any other drug that could kill her, while her parents were not consulted.'

Was there a Government inquiry? Was the 'Brooks' doctor who gave her the supplies reported to the General

Medical Council? Of course not! The Pill is sacred, and above reproach. 'Death by misadventure' said the Coroner, and under the carpet goes yet another, disposable young life.

I often ponder on what some people call 'failed parents'. Who *are* they exactly? I suppose all of us, if we cast our minds around for a few seconds, could come up with a suitably horrid case. We would imagine them to be working class, uneducated, irreligious, single parents or divorced and coming from the poorer end of town. We ourselves would never be included, naturally!

Would it surprise you to know that these assumptions had also crossed the minds of DHSS officials? Well they have. Back in 1979 I received a letter from a faceless DHSS civil servant who made it all perfectly clear to me who this contraceptive policy was aimed at:

'It is also, in the Government's view, a highly desirable social objective to remove the fear of unwanted pregnancy whenever it occurs. The Health and Social Services cannot close their eyes to the existence of extra-marital and pre-marital sexual relations. It is not to be taken as an indication of moral approval, nor as a diminution of the value attached to family life, that contraceptive advice is available to all who seek it. Indeed, many of the serious social problems of this age can be traced in one way or another to the lack of contraceptive knowledge or the availability of the means of contraception; for example, the problems of one-parent families and forms of economic and other deprivation which bring poverty, vandalism, delinquency and even crime in their wake.'

There you have it! The massacre at the Brussels football stadium in June, by young men, with enough spare cash to afford the fares all the way over and back, and all the drink in between, was not the result of violence in the terraces by nasty, comprehensively and contraceptively educated thugs – but the result of their mothers not having taken the Pill when they were unmarried teenagers! There are none so blind as bureaucrats, it seems, or so ridiculous. In all fairness though, the views of this insignificant DHSS bellboy were not original, for a former Shadow Home Secretary had said exactly the same things back in 1974. That was Sir Keith Joseph, who made such a remarkable speech in Birmingham in favour of free contraception for all, that the national dailies dubbed it as his 'Pills for the Proles' speech, in great glee.

The conclusions he drew and the solutions he proposed, left many people extremely angry and not a little fearful of things to come. He claimed that socio-economic groups 4 and 5 (a modern euphemism for the working class) were 'producing problem children, the future unmarried mothers, delinquents, denizens of our borstals and subnormal education establishments, prisons, hostels for drifters'. Because of these people, he said the 'balance of our population, our human stock, is threatened'.

How were we to break this 'cycle of deprivation' he asked? By extending birth control facilities to the young unmarrieds, he suggested. But was that not condoning immorality, he asked himself again? 'I suppose it is,' he answered, adding: 'But which is the lesser evil, until we are able to remoralise whole groups and classes of people, undoing the harm done when already weak restraints on strong instincts are further weakened by permissiveness in television, in films and on bookstalls?' Eleven years after that speech, he could have comfortably tacked onto that list: ' . . . and in schools and family planning clinics for teenagers . . . . '

So now I asked myself the simple question – 'Is we are, or is we ain't, a remoralised nation?' – since that 1974 call to contraception.

Are we all safer in our beds, so to speak (or on our streets, come to that) since we allowed every medical Tom, Dick and Harry to interfere with our children and the daily intimacies of family life?

Well, some of us are certainly *not*. The letter I received from a 'single-parent' in Kent, gave the lie to the notion that some people are automatically *uncaring* of their children. Some people certainly have special difficulties, no one would deny; but must they always be treated as

138

though they had no hearts to be hurt, and no children worthy of proper care and protection?

'Dear Victoria,
Please excuse the familiarity, but I feel that we must be soul sisters, except that I was not strong enough to take the steps that you have taken.

I have lived along with my daughter who is now 18, with another woman and her daughter B...., who is now 16, for the last thirteen years.

B.... always wanted to be older than her years, so that when she met this lad of 23, at a friend's family party, when she was 15 and a quarter years, and he paid special attention towards her, I could almost foresee what was going to happen. The boy irresponsibly fulfilled an impressionable teenager's desire for "love" and wrote a letter declaring his undying love, and from then on we had to fight to try and control this exploding situation.

When thwarted at home she ran around to his family and pleaded a tale of woe and they took her in. We tried to communicate, but were faced with an unintelligent response from a simple mother who couldn't understand our consternation.

The social workers were involved and B.... was found a safe place to lodge, but created a situation and took herself once again to the family of the lad. At this time we found that B.... was now on the Pill at 15 and a half years. When we confronted the doctor, his response was: 'Well what's best, to have illegitimate children or the Pill?'

The social worker's attitude was one of helplessness, with 16 looming so near, and the police didn't wish to know.

The point I am so long-windedly trying to communicate, is that I am so alarmed at "society's" ease in accepting such a calamity in a "child's" life and seems to be actively working against the parent.

B....'s mother and I are absolutely drained by these events, and completely puzzled that, as one-parent mums, we have struggled for so many years without assistance, to be so "insulted" in the end by our caring, responsible attitudes ripped from us.

B.... is now, at 16 years 1 month old, moving into a house with the lad!!!'

Now let us look at the 'loving, caring, stable family', so beloved by compassionate female journalists, when they are trying to describe those children who will *never* seek contraception. This kind of family is supposed to have dropped, complete, from Heaven; and is totally immune from the dangerous influences of the world outside.

A Lincolnshire mother wrote at length, about her own experience. She was a Christian and she was undoubtedly caring. But it didn't stop the clinic treating her as if she wasn't, and exacerbating the problems she already had with her daughter:

'The problem started when our daughter was 14 years old. We still don't know whether or not she was taking the Pill then; in fact we don't know when she first took it. This is the awful dilemma for parents. We *do* know our daughter was taking the Pill when she was 16 because my husband found them. We did not agree with her taking the Pill even at this age, she was too young, too immature to realise the physical damage the Pill could do; and the risk of cervical cancer because of promiscuity. Too young to cope with the emotional damage and upheaval in her young life, through being involved in so many short sexual affairs (as most of her relationships with boys seem to be). We could see her being used and then dropped, and each time she was hurt, upset, depressed, her school work suffered; the problems were endless.

In the meantime, before and after we found out that she was taking the Pill, I would talk to her about her relationships with boys, and tell her she didn't have to throw herself at boys, and that she would gain their respect if she said "no" to any demands for sex. But she seemed unwilling and incapable of saying no, and there are so many reasons for this I think. Easy

140

availability of the Pill. Most other peers were involved in sexual relationships, whether casually or at parties, at each other's homes when parents were out (these facts are true, our other children have said these things go on even in their peer group). It seems to be an accepted fact that if a teenage couple go out with each other for a few months, they start to have a sexual relationship. Girls feel it's their responsibility to take precautions (and boys accept this) and make themselves sexually prepared and available by taking the Pill (I believe in our case our daughter hoped that this would mean the boys would like her more and stay with her, but it often worked out the opposite).

The media, health services, TV, films etc., etc., all give the OK to sex, in and out of marriage, encourage teenage sex, and in fact discuss, show and talk about it far too much, and the young soon learn that sex is something to experiment with as *soon* as possible.

Our nation is no longer a Christian country; in fact it is almost a Godless nation, I'm so sad to say, and therefore Christian morals are no longer talked about or practiced, and again the younger generation miss out, they have no guidelines to help them. Also, for the parents who are Christian, it is an uphill struggle the whole time, for them, to try to teach and guide their own children, to ignore the massive tide of immorality, and to stick to Christian values and morals. Young, immature teenagers are soon following the mainstream unfortunately.

From the age of about 15, our daughter continually pestered to be allowed to go to more and more parties, and asked if she could stay the night at the homes of various friends (we trusted her until she was 16 and a half, when we found out she was on the Pill) so we allowed her to go to parties and stay out nights at the homes of friends, who either called or rang and told us their parents agreed.

Also, now and again, I would ring various parents to make sure they agreed, but found out later on a number of occasions that parents would be out until late, and parties were totally unsupervised. My daughter objected to me making 'phone calls, accused us of not trusting her, so I decided not to ring any more. But we later found out she abused our trust, time and time again.

It's so heartbreaking, when you bring your children up in a respectable Christian home, to find your daughter has done everything you would never have believed she would do. She was also drinking and smoking out of the home; we pointed out the dangers of both, but she continued behind our backs.

Arguments increased as she reached her 'O' Level year, because her social life took priority over her school work. All her teachers said she was capable of passing her 'O' Levels with good grades, if she applied herself to her homework and swotting (she took 8 Ordinary levels). However, we had a terrible time trying to get her to understand she couldn't go out as regularly as she wished. This affected the whole family, and made a very unhappy atmosphere for us all. She had an endless stream of boyfriends and yet we still didn't suspect anything.

During this time her health suffered, she had constant headaches, sleeping problems and kept feeling run down. I even went to the doctor with her once, to make sure he really took notice of what she said. In fact my daughter asked me to go with her, because when she went on her own, she didn't think they took her seriously. I was worried about her and it grieves me and angers me to think that the doctor probably knew she was on the Pill, and couldn't or wouldn't tell me. Also, for all I know, these health problems could have been caused by the Pill.

She only passed four 'O' levels, Grade C, and was very upset; but really we didn't expect any more, because she hadn't applied herself. Then she went to sixth form for one year, and it was a wasted, painful year for her and us. She was involved with one boyfriend after another; wanted to be out all the time; she played truant from school, so she could be with boyfriends, or out on the town with a group of her friends. Her reports were bad, and we were told she had days off regularly, and she told us she went to the homes of friends. Now all these friends come from respectable homes, many middle class families, with parents probably as much in the dark about things as we were.

Still, up to this point, we never thought our daughter was on the Pill or doing anything wrong. However, she had one boyfriend whom she really seemed to like and she became more demanding and wanted to stay out more and more (she was 17 then). We were angry when she stayed out nights and said she wasn't allowed to do this. Argument followed argument, and she left the sixth form mid-Easter term, as it was a waste of time her going there. We were very disappointed, because she had the potential to do well, but her mind was on other things.

Then she left home at 17 and a half; in fact she really ran away one evening after we said she must stay in one evening because she had been out continually. We had to think of the other children, and therefore we couldn't let her do as she pleased, when not yet 18, and we had to have rules, otherwise life would be chaos. All the children were expected to help with chores, but our daughter had no time to help with anything, and the younger ones said it wasn't fair because *she* always got away with things. So we had to enforce our rules, and we said our daughter should stay in and tidy her room. She escaped through the bedroom window and we didn't see her until next day; we were frantic with worry. She had been with her boyfriend, and the next day made arrangements to go and live in a flat with two other girls (all under 18). We could have stopped her because she was under 18, but we decided not to, because she was 17 and a half and would soon be 18, and matters were bad enough. We were exhausted by this time.

She left home so she could see this boy whenever she wanted to, night and day. He finished with her 2 months later. She lived in squalor for 3 months. She lost a lot of weight and looked so ill, and lived with two punk girls, and we were *very* worried about her. She became very depressed and we were terrified she would turn to drugs; we heard via friends that she had tried them.

I thank God for the prayers of my Christian friends, because I *know* prayer saved her. I managed to rally her a little, and got her a place at the Technical College on a two-year course. She had to come back home (thank God) because she was refused a grant; so her father said he would provide for her.

I had to nurse her back to health again; she was a physical and emotional wreck, and was on the verge of anorexia; a nurse friend of mine told me how to deal with her.

My daughter was so hurt that this boyfriend had finished with her when she had done all she could for him, including leaving her home and living on social security. She grieved for this boyfriend more than any other, and this took its toll on her health.

However, thank God she gradually recovered. In the meantime we found out about her being on the Pill since she was 14, and about her various sexual relationships. I'm sure you can understand as you read this letter, that the misuse of sex by teenagers can lead to *so* many problems for them and others too.

Our problems could go on, as well, because she refuses to have a cervical smear test; the doctor hasn't mentioned to her that she should have one. I've tried to persuade her, but she won't, even though she has had problems from a very heavy discharge and has been treated with pessaries recently. The long term physical effects; well we just hope she doesn't suffer any of them.

I hope this brief letter of what we suffered, because of the permissive, sexual freedom encouraged amongst teenagers today, may help you *warn* others of the many dangers and pitfalls and heartache involved.

It maybe an uphill struggle, but we Christian parents *must* do something to stem this abnoxious tide from overwhelming our present immature and vulnerable teenage generation. Giving the Pill to the promiscuous minority encourages the majority to experiment with sex, and all the time at a younger age.

144

She is 20 this year, and intends leaving home when she has finished her course. She has matured a little, but all we can do is let her go and pray that she doesn't always have to learn the hard way.'

Perhaps some people, reading her letter, will wonder how it was that the girl's parents suspected nothing for so long? But if you have shown love and trust to your children, why should you not expect that it is being returned in kind? Discos and parties can be great fun, but they can also be disastrous places for girls to meet the most unsuitable boys. Mass produced junk music, like junk food, can be a danger to health, both in mind and body! Maybe we parents ought to be considering reintroducing the idea of a 'chaperone' for our more wilful daughters. Maybe it is *we* who ought to be brave enough to say *no* occasionally to our daughters; and not leave them to fight all their battles on their own. It is a cruelty indeed, to expect duties of those too young to fulfil them.

But since that mother's troubles began six years ago, in 1979, it could be that, *at that time*, nobody really knew that doctors were getting so involved in the secret sex lives of other people's children. If it didn't occur to this family, one wonders how many thousands of other parents have been so wrongfully deceived over the past eleven years, since this invidious policy was secretly introduced?

Should we say that such suffering is neither here nor there, amidst the general aim of preventing pregnancies? Shall we hastily apportion blame to salve our consciences, and pass on to more obvious 'hard cases'?

Another inside view of how this policy is working amongst hardpressed families, came from a Northampton mother in November 1984. She wrote:

'I too had similar problems on a personal scale with my younger daughter, J.... when she was 15. She met a man six years older than herself, at a disco, and they began an affair long before her 16th birthday. I found the contraceptive pills one day on her dressing table when cleaning her bedroom, in open view, which made me think she wanted me to know about it. I talked to

145

her about the dangers of taking it over the long term, of beginning on an adult relationship when she was still a child, of the dangers to her health and to her barely developed body, *ad infinitum*. I even invited the man in question to have a chat about it, but all I got from him was the fact that *she* wanted it. He even took her to the Family Planning Clinic to fetch the pills. Nothing I could say would alter her attitude that I was old-fashioned and they wanted to have sex and there was nothing I could do about it.

Frankly, I was brokenhearted. She grew into a brash, cocksure little woman overnight, who talked openly of sex and behaved in an overtly sexual way in front of me. I cut pieces out of papers about the inherent dangers of the Pill for young girls, and left them for her to read; she threw them away and ridiculed me for my out-of-date standards.

I rang the Family Planning Clinic and asked to speak to the doctor in charge of her case (J.... did tell me that she had gone one evening with a friend and had been handed a plastic bag containing a six months' supply of the Pill without any medical examination being made, only a few facts checked verbally; even she was surprised at the ease with which she obtained them). The doctor was not available so I wrote a strong letter to her, but got no reply. I did manage to speak to another doctor eventually, and she was sympathetic and said she had children of the same age and knew how worried I would be. She promised to pass on my observations to the original doctor, but I never did get a reply.

All the while I had to deal with this challenging rebellious child (for that is all she is) who knew there was not a thing I could do about it. We had lulls in this warfare when she would seem to see reason, and would promise to give up the Pill and having sex at least for a spell, but the man in question obviously put pressure on her and she would resume taking it. I tried everything, talking to her like an adult, ignoring it for a spell, coming the heavy mother, the lot – result stale-mate.

146

By now she was 16 and legally able to do as she wished and I gave up. She threatened to leave home often, to get a flat with her boyfriend; I did try to stay on good terms with him through all this, because he really is quite a decent fellow, fortunately. But it was all a bitter disappointment to me, I must admit, and the relationship interfered with her school work, so she failed her 'O' Levels and her health suffered. She even developed thrush last Christmas and I thought that might shame her into abstaining until she was older, when the doctor chastised her, but no.

I am a single parent, which has made the whole affair more difficult to handle because I feel, had I had support from her father, she might have listened to reason. However, he is afraid of losing her affection, so shrugged the whole thing off, when I asked for his back-up. This, in fact made it worse because she now had her father and her boyfriend lined up against me. In fact, looking back, it was a much harder thing to cope with than my actual divorce, and one of my biggest heartaches.

She is still with this boyfriend after all this while, which is to her credit, and planning to leave home soon anyway, so my battle is lost. But I hope you succeed where others failed to get the pernicious law rescinded. It strikes at the heart of the family because it diminishes the status of the parent and gives the girl powers beyond her capability. I know my daughter is still very young at heart, but feels that she is now adult because she is having sex with her boyfriend in spite of (and there's the crunch) all my advice. At this age children challenge their parents' authority anyway; now they have support from outside to flaunt their standards and principles. She was far too young mentally, emotionally and physically to embark on an adult relationship at 15. Perhaps in years to come she will realise I was right.'

It may be appropriate at this moment to quote from the report on the working of the 'Young Persons Advisory Clinic' which was set up in *Northamptonshire* amidst a blaze of adverse publicity in 1983. It was established to give a counselling service directed towards young people of both sexes 'from puberty to 18 or the age of school leaving', it said. Unlike some people, they were honest enough to refer to the children as 'clients' and not 'patients'.

All clients, without exception they said, are advised to discuss contraception with their parents: 'Where this has presented difficulties, it has been suggested that this was easiest done by leaving some FPA leaflets around the home to provoke discussion.'

Information about the clinic had been 'disseminated through schools, lectures to church groups, teachers, social workers and police staff and through health clinics and health professionals. The Authority's Health Education Department produced and distributed posters for the clinic'. It was intended in the future 'to make increased use of health education materials and to hold discussions in the clinic involving teachers from various schools'.

The result of this approach? I quote:- 'Many clients come with a group of friends who are also invited to discuss how they heard about the clinic and whether they are also in need of advice. Advantage is taken of these 'captive audiences' because it has sometimes been obvious that one person has come forward to test the facilities offered. Through this kind of approach, a trust is built up and other members of the group have appeared in later weeks seeking advice.'

During their first six months in 1983 fifty eight of 116 new contacts were girls seeking oral contraception, eleven were supplied with barrier methods; thirteen for pregnancy tests.

The report had to 'admit that' a large number of girls attended to seek facts about contraception', then added: 'Attendance at a clinic for these young people is a very responsible act and should be encouraged.' To this end they were prepared to provide 'a confidential and non-judgemental contact with the clinic. In some instances this might mean providing underage girls who are at risk with initial supplies of contraceptives.'

(Is this what they meant, when they gave a plastic bag containing six months' supply of the Pill to the 15 year old daughter of the Northampton mother whose letter I have just included?) Contrasted with this 'non-judgemental' approach to giving a pubescent girl a powerful and dangerous hormone drug for her hazardous sexual activity, is the report's harsh and moralistic tone regarding mere smoking: 'The clinic team feel it is important that we are consistent with our message on the dangers of smoking and that smoking is abnormal and unacceptable.'

Parents and teachers in Northampton will also be glad to know that in 1983 this clinic, for the part-time schoolgirl, was considering opening its doors to them at *lunchtime* as well as in the evening. Happily for everyone involved, some kind soul had also brought it to the clinic staff's attention that 'some young people may be in need of spiritual guidance'. Did they perhaps feel their *spirits* needed contraceptive counselling as well? Comforting, isn't it? . . . .

A typical birth control nurse wrote to me in 1985. At least, I presume that she would like to be considered typical, and not a freak. She was quite young and had a couple of little children, and any number of jolly good ideas about what makes adolescents tick and how to be a responsible parent for ever and ever. She hadn't worked in this country for long, but seemed to think that her African experience would fit the British bill anyhow.

As you read the following extract from her slight, trite, facile, but tediously long exhortation, please bear in mind the letters you have just read from 'hard case' mothers and their problems; and don't be surprised at her personal comments about myself: most people in birth control practise are only doing the job because they are so very, very sensitive and non-judgemental about other people's choices! And she did work for the International Planned Parenthood Federation after all . . . .

'I believe in emphasis being placed on responsible parenthood which, in itself, envelops all kinds of factors – family size, rearing, feeding and so forth as well as the parents themselves creating the rôle model for the child. A child of say 15, who goes to her GP or

149

clinic for FP does so, because she is sexually active. Why she became active at that young age is a result of many things – rebellion, poor parental care, peer group pressure and so forth. Whether you can *stop her* from continuing her sexual activity is not the duty of the health worker, nor can the HW do any more than advise her against this, if she is doing it without any consideration etc., etc. A stable happy home tends to include healthy, open relationships between parents and their young, though not always. What I and various colleagues don't understand, is why you should be so concerned about your own daughters? Has there been a severe breakdown in communications, or what? Why should you be so concerned about them – so much so that you have endeavoured all these years to have the law changed? Do you consider yourself "average" or are you one of the privileged, educated middleclass minority?

I really don't want it to appear like I am attacking you (!) but I find it hard to appreciate how a woman who has had ten children in the 1980s can preach "responsible parenthood".

I *do* agree with you that there is abuse and that the system does not work perfectly. If a girl however, becomes sexually active below 16, there is usually a good reason, and many of these girls are most likely to come from less-privileged backgrounds in which they would find it very hard to raise a child and provide a child with its basic human rights. What we need to attack is poverty, lack of education etc., etc.

To that, I say that *no* child, conceived with a human soul, in the image and likeness of its creator is born a 'hard case'. But lies, deception, folly and medical neglect or abuse, can make them so. The way back to a more honest and genuinely compassionate society that does not allow its professional classes to back-off from their moral responsibilities, or substitute chemicals for care, is going to be a long, hard haul. It cannot begin soon enough.

Eight: 'A Statement of Faith'

Following our initial defeat in the High Court in 1983 and
the tremendous Public Petition to the House of Commons
in the late autumn of that year, there followed a year of in-
tense political and media activity. It was 'Orwell's year' –
1984. The significance of it was not missed in some
quarters, as gloomy forebodings of a second defeat in the
Appeal Court at the hands of 'Big Brother' grew apace.

For my own part, I have always subscribed to the idea
that the best form of defence is attack; and happily
commented to one and all, that Women's Lib had
changed Orwell's predictions in one vital respect: From
now on it was to be 'Big Mother' who was watching *them*!

I've never known such a time of cut and thrust between
two opposing forces.

Of course the media loved every minute of it. Meat and
drink to them: feed them a good juicy story, with all the
best ingredients of sex and political intrigue, and they are
hooked!

Now, I don't mean to be cynical, but let's be honest,
news *is* part of the entertainment industry. It is also
usually about conflict of one sort or another: either wars,
strikes, street brawls, marital infidelities, race riots,
competitive sports and political shenanigans. In our case
the conflict involved parents at odds with State
officialdom and the birth-controllers. What was more, it
was about *SEX*. Better still, it was *under age* sex. As some
journalists so warmly commented: 'This one will run and
run . . . .'

Nor was the media – or most of it – particularly
biased one way or another, as far as I could tell.
Occasionally, a producer displayed a personal antipathy
to anything that stood in the way of birth prevention
policies. But they were few in number.

Of course, when a news item or article appeared which

151

seemed overwhelmingly to support our 'opponents' there were those who wrote to me complaining that everything was all unfairly one sided. Sometimes it did seem a little too blatant; but on the whole it was just part of the media technique of keeping a good conflict going – not very moral; but no more than we have come to expect.

Not that this Saga needed such artificial props, however. It had a very definite life of its own, and an urgency about it, which drew almost everybody concerned to a daily ringside seat watching the bitter tussle of the combatants in the ring.

Perhaps some people still think that it would have been so much better if left well alone. It distressed them to see such a private and delicate matter, involving children, decked out in dirty linen and paraded for all to gawp at.

But from our point of view – and by 'our' I mean all of us who had spent so many precious years, throwing good writing paper at an indolent and indifferent DHSS, only to receive standardised word-processor replies – this *public* fight was the best thing to happen in years! At last – at long, long last, we had dragged these faceless policy-makers out of their conspiratorial back rooms, and into the ring of public debate. Though, naturally enough, we never managed to get the officials themselves to do the fighting. They used their fall-guys to take the knocks on their behalf. It was the BMA and the General Medical Council who usually swapped verbal blows with the mothers of the country; and received bloody noses for their trouble!

Nor was the BMA slow in coming forward. It was almost embarrassing the way in which it kept throwing itself frenetically on to the mat, in its efforts to protect its members' interests, during 1984 and 1985.

For example, they knew that our case, having been lost in the High Court, would be Appealed within a few months. What they *didn't* know – any more than we did – was when that day would be. So they simply kept on firing off their big propaganda guns, every time they thought it was about to come to Court and they reckoned they might have a chance to influence the Judges. And each time they had the humiliating experience of having to sit back and watch, while their salvoes vanished ineffectually over the horizon, as the predicted date came and went, and no Appeal was announced.

First it was Christmas 1983; then the following February; until by Easter 1984 they were beside themselves with 'press conference' gloom and despondency; announcing their absolute certainty in a return to back-street abortions, suicidal girls, rocketing pregnancy rates and festering, untreated venereal diseases, should the Appeal find in favour of parental responsibility.

Even Lord Denning thought their tactics were just 'not cricket', and deplored the way in which a powerful and wealthy trade union such as the BMA should use its resources to attack an individual whose court case was still pending.

When the BMA actually named him as being one of *their* chief supporters, he was most incensed and denied it hotly, which was most encouraging.

It was probably around this time, that the BMA officials began seriously to lose a number of their friends in the media. BMA faces were grim; their message was grimmer. Yet at the same time they seemed to offer no solution or hope for the future. They just wanted to be allowed to poddle along in the same old way as before. But as many people had by now noticed – they had been poddling along the same old track for the last 10 years, quite unopposed, and look where it had taken the rest of us!

There were now thousands upon thousands of once healthy adolescent girls, giving themselves dangerous daily doses of hormone steroids, and yet the teenage pregnancy rate had been steadily rising since 1980, while abortion numbers had doubled. Sexual diseases, once the painful lot of ageing prostitutes, were now running at epidemic levels in the classroom. Child abuse and incest had grown yearly more common; and lunchtimes in some cities were plagued with primary and secondary school-children plying their sexual wares on the streets in the oldest and ugliest trade of all. And all the BMA could suggest was to give yet more and more of these young tragedies more hormone pills!

153

It was during these first weeks of 1984, and whilst some of the Public Petitions were still arriving in the House of Commons from Northern Ireland and elsewhere, that it occurred to me that not *everyone* had been given a chance to voice their opinion on this issue. There were the West Indians, Asians and Muslims, whose opinions on matters of morality never seem to be included in any public debate. By all accounts, they had very strong views indeed on family life and children; why not ask them? So I did. The result was truly wonderful. Not only were they very much opposed to the DHSS guidelines on contraception and young girls, but they were also extremely aware of what was happening in society around them; and even resented bitterly the way in which their own communities were often regarded quite *indiscriminately* as totally hopeless cases, incapable of civilised values, or yearnings towards a better way of life, as were the rest of us. Yet, as far as I could see, we were all in the same sinking boat together.

The letter from the secretary of the Afro-Asian-Caribbean Standing Committee on Merseyside, who was also a college lecturer and magistrate, was most cheering, seeing as it seemed to indicate that we were not alone in thinking that amoral sex education was a primary problem for many parents:

'Dear Mrs Gillick,
I am delighted that you had such an astounding success in your campaign against parental rights being whittled away by Government legislation, which is harmful to the nation as a whole.

It hits at the very root and concept of the family life, which should be protected responsibly, first by parents then by other voluntary and statutory child care agencies.

In my view, the dividing line between the childhood and the adulthood at the age of 16 is rather flimsy.

Sex education and the type of sex education with all the practical ornaments of sexual activity is most undesirable. We oppose such education. We endorse wholeheartedly all your work and give our support to help you in saving society from the disastrous consequences.

Administration of contraception and consent to abort must remains the concern of the parents, not the doctors alone. By giving doctors such medication rights, it opens the door for free sex and eventually thousands of one-parent families – a growing menace and burden to the ratepayer. Our organisation stands by you and we pray that you may succeed.

Yours sincerely
Syed Safiruddin
(Secretary).'

I actually had an opportunity to meet Mr Safiruddin on a Tyne Tees Television programme in January of 1985. He was part of the audience in a very lively and heated debate on this very issue, and made an extremely telling point, when he was given the opportunity to speak. He said that those who advocated sex for young girls were hypocrites, because he was aware that Muslims such as he were often criticised by Europeans for their tradition of early marriages. If a Muslim girl married at, say, 14 or 15 that was considered backward and primitive; but if they simply had sex at that age it was regarded as perfectly all right! An irrefutable observation.

From the West Indian Standing Conference in London, came an equally supportive response:

'Dear Mrs Gillick,
Your clarification that the issue in question has to do with the giving of contraceptives to girls under the age of 16 enabled a resumption of the debate at the Monthly General Meeting of Delegates of the Conference held yesterday, Sunday 5th March 1984.

You will be pleased to hear that the decision was reached to give support to your campaign that young girls under the age of consent (16 years) should not be prescribed contraceptives without consultation with the parents.

Regard was had to the real situation where young

155

girls in particular are greatly influenced to rebel against their parents by outside attractions and where, in the majority of cases, they would leave the family unit to set up house and become mothers in a quite unprepared and inexperienced state.

The West Indian Standing Conference has always been strongly opposed to much of what has been allowed to develop over recent years to reduce progressively the influence and authority of parents over their children.

The Conference wishes the campaign every success.
Yours sincerely
W. I. TRANT
Director
Admin. Programme & Field Services

It wasn't just the 'comfortable English middle class' who were upset at what has been happening to the young over the last couple of decades. *Everyone* could see it, and everybody was being affected by it.

The one group of people whom one might have thought were not directly involved in all this sexual and moral mayhem were the Muslims. Yet they too, for all the strength of their religion and family ties, were feeling the strain. For example, an educational system, which purports to be directed towards a multi-ethnic pluralism in its social education, and yet which still manages to leave those of a specific faith somehow deeply dissatisfied.

So, from the Union of Muslim Organisations of UK and Eire, I was not really surprised, though deeply grateful, to receive the following beautiful letter:

'Dear Mrs Gillick,
Thank you for your letters of the 1st December 1983 and 7th February 1984, with enclosures. As I promised over the telephone, I brought this matter before our Executive Committee and a full discussion has taken place on several aspects concerning parental rights which have been mentioned in your letter of 1st December.

As you know, Islam is strict in the observance of the moral code as delineated in the Holy Qur'an, which is the literal word of Almighty Allah, and the Sunnah, which are traditions of our holy prophet Muhammad, peace and blessings of Almighty Allah be on him. Under this divine moral code sexual relations must be confined within the institution of marriage. Secondly, the parents are under an obligation to nurture their children in accordance with this divine moral code right from childhood. Islam not only forbids the commission of a sin, but also forbids all actions which lead to the commission of this sin. Respect for parents constitutes an essential part of a Muslim child's behavioural pattern. A tradition of our holy prophet says that Paradise lies at the feet of mothers. It is this twin concept of fear of Almighty Allah and obedience to parents that has enabled the Muslim community to retain its moral standards over the centuries. Added to this is the fact that boys and girls are not allowed to mix freely and early marriages are preferred in cases of sexually active children.

Having said this, I am coming to the specific point raised in your letter, i.e. Section G of the DHSS Health Notice of 1980 which advises doctors that they may prescribe contraceptive drugs or devices to girls under the Age of Consent, without consulting their parents. We strongly oppose this statute and demand its repeal as it tends to undermine the Right of Parents to maintain morality and chastity of their daughters. It is also dangerous because it encourages both boys and girls to rebel against their parents. As you have rightly stated in your letter this statute gives a licence to mischief mongers to exploit teenagers for their personal gain. Therefore, we strongly support your campaign to have this statute abrogated through an Act of Parliament.

Yours sincerely,
Dr Syed Aziz Pasha
General Secretary.'

It certainly makes me very sad at the way some Christian Churches and many Christians themselves are so hesitant about their faith, and reluctant to admit it with pride, in any public forum. When did you ever hear a Muslim apologise for his faith? That letter gave me great confidence against those who would vilify my own Faith, or pour scorn upon it, as they once did upon its Founder, two thousand years ago.

I particularly liked the Muslim tradition of paradise 'lying at the feet of mothers'. As a Catholic, I have always learned that supplication at the feet of the Mother of Christ was a sure way to the Mind of God.

Modern 'ecumenism' seems to have been concerning itself with all the wrong issues and has got itself entangled with 'religion' and has somehow forgotten that within all mankind there is a common thread of understanding and agreement. Man's true nature and the natural law is the common ingredient. Stay with that, and we will find those fundamental universal principles, upon which true Unity is based.

Prejudice of one sort or another is usually supposed to come from extreme 'right wing' organisations. But there is a covert prejudice amongst the respectable members of the Establishment, which is far more devastating in the long run, in that it is *these* people who ultimately make the Rules by which we are governed – or I should say, controlled.

As long ago as 1981, I had written to the Secretary of State for Social Services, and declared my belief that it was becoming increasingly clear to everyone, that the DHSS policies on family planning and overall population control, were an attempt by the State at a form of social engineering. In the firing line were certain religious, racial and social groups, and I warned that such divisive policies would only cause social anarchy and a growing division between the generations, and between the rulers and the ruled. I believed even then as now, that as a result, the rôles of parenthood, motherhood and fatherhood would be devalued in the eyes of the younger generation. I nailed my flags to the mast and said that from then on I would never cease to oppose them in what they were, so unwisely, seeking to achieve.

I doubted whether any modern government would have either the wit or the wisdom to cope with the results of these socially dangerous policies, in the years ahead, in any recognisably civilised or humanitarian way.

We know now that 'uncivilised' methods were already happening, as more and more instances of pressurised or compulsory sterilisations come to light, and the abortions and injected contraceptives, which unwitting women and girls have had perpetrated upon them, when they are quite unable to comprehend the full nature of what is being done – 'in the best interests of society', of course!

With ten children myself, and being one of a religious minority in England, I have become increasingly aware of what it feels like to be regarded as a social pariah or an oddity, in some sections of our beloved liberal press.

Thus it came as no great surprise to me, to find that even in the General Medical Council itself, there were those permanent officials who were tarred with this prejudicial brush. In August 1983, just one month after our High Court failure, I telephoned a senior official at GMC headquarters in London. I was determined to say my piece, as a concerned mother, about their newly published rules, which removed from doctors their right to exercise a time-honoured and wise procedure, of always involving parents in any consultation with their young children. Because of these new rules, they had now been forbidden to do so when dealing with abortion and contraception in underage girls. From now on, they had to obey the dictums and directions of a mere child, and keep silent or face disciplinery action by the GMC.

'Good grief, what are you playing at!' I almost shouted down the telephone receiver. In something of a fluster he explained that the GMC was under a lot of pressure from the DHSS to introduce these rules. And anyway, he added, as if to excuse himself, they weren't meant to apply to ordinary families, but for those in the inner city areas. 'You mean immigrants?' I challenged. 'Well,' he admitted, 'I'm not a racist – but we do have problems . . . .'

That was the first time I had ever heard official policy stated quite so unambiguously – if a little unwisely.

It may well be true, that cities have far greater social

problems than do towns or country areas. Yet I would have thought it was obvious enough, that in a country which claims 'equality under the law', you cannot remove from one section of the population legal protection and parental rights, without eventually having to remove everyone else's as well.

It is also apparent that any such devious attempts to do so will ultimately come unstuck. Children are not the only ones who know when they are not wanted: adults know it too! Nor does such an attitude by government encourage peaceful co-existence or improve social harmony. Like unwanted children, unwanted adults can become very disruptive and anarchistic. They can even topple the very social order upon which the State and good government itself depends for its own continuing existence; let alone the survival of its citizens.

Steering a course between two extreme options is the task of a civilised and democratic government: on the one extreme they can go all out for *laissez-faire* and letting the weak go to the wall; or they can do the other thing and take complete control of everyone.

These DHSS guidelines on birth control for the young may appear, at face value, to be an altruistic attempt by the State to create a safety net for the wayward. In reality, they were the means by which others (either for idealistic or financial considerations) caused social mayhem and an ultimate attempt at total state control.

This is why the DHSS is so determined not to lose the case which I brought against them. They cannot, they *will* not let go of the reins of social control, once they have them in hand. But the independence of the family as a social institution is crucial in any truly free society; which is why every tyrant that has ever existed, has always set out first to break up the family. 'Divide and conquer' it is usually called.

Although I still have great faith in the commonsense of the British public and their naturally independent spirit, I can also sympathise with those whose memories are longer than mine, and who are deeply fearful of the way in which our modern governments are currently manipulating social policies. A Catholic priest from West

Lothian wrote to me after the 1983 court case and said:

'You have our prayers in your battle which is ours, for the family versus the State. The State won in Russia and Nazi Germany – isn't it odd no one seems to notice this drift to totalitarianism!'

The same sentiments, but expounded at greater length, came in a statement from an Anglican minister:

'The Christian Church regards the family as the natural cell of human social life. The function of the State or of the municipality or the professions is to uphold and strengthen it, not to try to usurp its place.

The natural guardians of children below physical and mental maturity are their parents: And the place of national or local authorities and of doctors or other professional persons is to be the pilot called to the bridge by the captain; not to be usurper captains.

Some parents have, no doubt, failed in their duties; but so have some public authorities and professional persons. The evidence of their performance gives them no greater claim to infallibility than that of parents, most of whom show responsibility.

Further, in prescribing contraceptives for a girl under sixteen without the knowledge of her parents, the doctor's estimate of the parents would in most cases rest on the unsupported impression of them, given by the girl herself.

The decision to allow doctors so to behave is likely to encourage the minority of parents who find their responsibility irksome and are glad to push it on to an anonymous "them", at the expense of undermining the proper authority of the majority of parents, who find their dignity in its proper and loving exercise. It is more in line with right or left wing totalitarianism than with democracy.'

We are sometimes apt to forget, or even to dismiss, the feelings of those who are not themselves married or parents. Nevertheless they still feel very acutely, that something has gone fundamentally awry within society. Being a part of the community, they suffer like the rest of us, and feel shame for their countrymen, when they see all around, the God-given gift of sexual attraction and procreation, debased and debauched at all levels and in every age group.

Eighteen nuns from Dorset wrote to me in 1983 expressing their own great distress at what has happened to the young in recent years:

> 'It was with a sense of deep shock that we read of the failure of the High Court case about contraceptives for girls under 16. It is a terrible slur on our country that such a decision should be made. Still more is it a grievous offence against the Law of God.
>
> We are an enclosed community and so cannot offer you active support, but we should like you to know we stand firmly behind you and support you with our prayers.
>
> May God give you courage and strength to fight on and may He bless your efforts. We share, too, your anxiety for your own children and will keep them in our prayers.'

But to return to the tussles of 1984. Early in the year, it occurred to some of us, who were trying hard to put our case against the DHSS in broader and more explicit terms, that we ought to follow the example of the Victorian social reformer, Josephine Butler, and her 'Ladies National Association', and petition the Prime Minister herself. It was for this reason that the Salvation Army, Valerie Riches of 'Family and Youth Concern' and myself, drew up a declaration which explained in some detail our present concern with the Government's current policy on birth control for girls under 16.

We followed the reasoning of Josephine Butler very closely, as it seemed that, in 1869, women were battling against the same kind of political intransigence and blinkered vision that we were witnessing in our own times.

One hundred and twenty professional women, in

teaching, medicine, law, journalism and the arts, all signed this 'Women's Protest' and it was duly handed in to No 10.

It was such an excellent resumé of all our arguments that I include it in full at the back of this book, in the Appendix.

Although we hoped it would set some people thinking in the Cabinet, we received no more than an 'official' reply to it.

From then on hardly a month went by without some group or other lunging into the fray, earnestly exhorting the public – or specific readers – to 'take urgent action!' for or against Gillick.

In March, the Communist newspaper *The Morning Star* carried an anti-Gillick article, edited by Ms Mikki Doyle on behalf of 'Doctors for a Woman's Choice on Abortion', with information supplied by the Birth Control Campaign (from their headquarters in the offices of the Family Planning Association).

April saw two other notable events: the first being an overwhelming vote in favour of the 'parents'-right-to-know' at the AGM of the National Council of Women's Associations. An amendment to the original proposal had initially been rejected. This amendment had been put forward by the FPA, and called for an exemption to be made, whereby doctors should be allowed to give secret contraception to girls being sexually abused by their fathers – contraception for child incest!

The will of the majority was finally thwarted when, on the last day of their meeting, the Central Committee voted in *favour* of ratifying the vote taken on the central issue; but not by a full two thirds majority, and the whole proposal was thereby dropped.

The second event was the breathtaking appearance outside No 10 of twenty four Agony Aunts. Once again the Family Planning Association was the organiser of their petition, which supported the DHSS guidelines. Unlike the 'Women's Protest', this one had widespread media coverage. Not surprising really; after all, Agony Aunts and their rather explicit correspondence pages, are part of the world of popular entertainment for most people.

On a lunchtime TV news item, between myself and one of these 'Agonies', Anna Raeburn (whose speciality in advice-giving includes her own radio programme on sex therapy), I accused her of being part of the problem – not part of the solution.

A gentleman from Hampshire seemed to feel the same way as I about these Aunties when he wrote to me, shortly afterwards:

'There are, I believe, millions in this country, who would like to see the nation set on firmer spiritual, moral and ethical grounds, where agony aunt opinion is swallowed by its own foundation of shifting sand; where those elected to authority serve the true interests of the people and where the sanctity of the family is afforded the protection and position it deserves.

During that short, sharp television scuffle, I couldn't help wondering out loud what the Minister for Health, in a Tory government, thought about his strange assortment of followers:- the officials of a medical trade union, the Communist Party, and 24 Agony Aunts! Did he have all the right political friends, I wondered?

Soft July brought not only 'apricots and gilly flowers', but also the annual BMA conference. At one of their daily press conferences, an unfortunate choice of words by the Chairman of the Ethical Committee, Dr Alexander Macara, brought reporters eagerly crowding round him. 'Doctors should not shop girls who come to them for contraceptives,' he said.

'Shop' girls? I thought it was only criminals who 'shopped' one another. His phrase caused quite a storm.

It was also suggested at that unhappy conference, that a doctor who refused to supply such contraceptive drugs to a child, would be breaking his terms of contract with the NHS. Thus doctors had been reduced to the level of shopkeepers, with the customer – a child – always in the right.

A mother from Colchester wrote to me about this time, concerning the 'Agony Aunts':

164

'I have often wished to give you my moral support but did not know where to write. What has really prompted me to do so now was reading how 10 professional women (including Claire Rayner, who ought to know better) are upholding the decision of doctors to prescribe contraceptives to underage children without informing their parents. The whole problem is being tackled at the wrong end by the authorities. They assume that the *status quo* is a normal one and that because under-age sex is widely practiced, it is therefore right and proper. It is being practiced, I believe, because it is being taught explicitly in schools, on TV, in the daily papers, in films, in fact everywhere, and because it has been completely divorced from love and marriage. In fact, I am not really against pre-marital sex. After all, it has always been done, though not on the present scale, and one has to admit that it has all the excitement of forbidden fruit! The great danger of the ruling about contraceptives is that children have now become chattels of the Government, and all parental responsibility has been taken away. Human nature, being what it is, this attitude is on the increase in all fields. We are now being protected from ourselves in many different ways. We have seat belts to protect us when we drive. The anti-smoking campaign is also being hotted up. We no longer have any responsibility for our old people, who can be taken care of in homes. And so on. The incentives to help ourselves and our children have gone, and so long as others will do it for us, we allow them to do so. It is so much of a struggle to fight against the system that many of us give up. We seem to spend our lives protesting about this and that, and getting nowhere.'

Now, I can't help thinking, that when people refer to all the follies and foibles of mankind, they really ought to remember that this is not just 'human nature' at work, but man's 'fallen' nature in action. When we behave as our Creator originally intended us to, as a species even, only then are we 'truly human'. Once you concede the

165

argument that *sin* is the true state of man's being, any attempt to distinguish between bad and not-so-bad sin, merely becomes an exercise in aesthetics. Like beauty, corruption itself becomes something little more than a squint in the eye of the beholder; and your case is a lost one.

September, and the answer to a Parliamentary Question, on the number of girls attending NHS clinics, elicited the reply that in 1983 there were 16,963 girls requesting the Pill – not many? Perhaps. But it was more than double the number of such girls in 1976. However, these figures still did not take into account those girls who went to their own GP for contraception.

Earlier in the year, a reputable medical survey of doctors revealed that 68% of them believed they saw *two* girls, for contraception, a year. The others reckoned they saw between 6 and a dozen girls in that time. If we take the lowest number of 2 per year, it doesn't sound very many, does it? Not until we realise that there are around 30,000 GPs in this country, does it begin to look like an alarming figure. Eighty thousand girls on the Pill! Surely not? And costing the NHS, £8.55 a year, plus the price of the drug itself. It must run into millions of pounds annually.

On top of that, there is the cost of VD treatment for teenagers; cervical cancer smears and treatment; abortions and illegitimate babies for pay for. All in all, it would seen to be an expensive business, giving teenagers their right to sexual expression.

But at least it does explain why some cancer specialists are getting grey hairs, trying to cope with the explosion of cervical cancers in younger and younger women; and why the pregnancy figures for the under sixteens, simply won't drop below certain levels, but seem instead, to be rising each year. Inexperienced troops always means more casualties in the end.

All these facts, and much else besides, came out in the controversial booklet around that time, by the 'Family and Youth Concern' organisation, and called 'No Entry for Parents'.

Once again, it brought weeping and wailing and

gnashing of teeth from family planners, who rent their garments, at such a calumny against their overworked and caring contraceptive counsellors.

As facts and figures were bandied about, proving or disproving this or that theory, a vicar from Somerset sent me a letter of his, which *The Times* had declined to publish:

> 'What sort of parents are we supposed to be? Damn the statistics; would Dr Havard's reaction, supposing him to have under-age daughters, be any different from mine, one of horror and outrage, if they were to be prescribed the contraceptive pill without his knowledge or consent?
>
> It simply will not do to take shelter behind a smokescreen of confidentiality (something, incidentally, about which, as a priest, I know). Either I am a responsible parent, in which case I utterly refute the right of anyone to keep from me the intention to prescribe the Pill (or anything else) without my knowledge and consent; or I am an irresponsible parent, in which case the Law can place my children in the care of others *in loco parentis* – which I take to mean exactly what it says.
>
> In all reverence, I thank God that both my daughters are of an age to be out of the influence, to exercise which, Dr Havard maintains his right. I rejoice that they have elected to marry and to raise their own families. But I tremble for their daughters, should they have them, if in the meantime the Law concerning the age of consent to such treatment has not been emphatically and unambiguously defined in the manner which has been supported already by hundreds of thousands of caring and responsible parents.'

In a sense, 1984 was the 'Year of the Media', for our campaign, and the spectacle of the 'big battalions' at loggerheads, which held the public's attention.

By October, I had decided to write to the Chief Rabbi, Sir Immanuel Jakobovits, and ask him for his own views on this thorny issue. A most inspiring answer came back, not only giving his wholehearted support, but also suggesting that a 'Public Statement' should be written and undersigned by all Religious and Community Leaders.

At once, I set to work composing such a statement, with the help and advice of a Midlands doctor. I felt absolutely sure that such a statement, that gathered us all together in unity, was not only very possible, but also very necessary. There was an urgent need to refute the humanist propaganda that my concern was simply an attempt by a quirky religious nutcase to impose her outdated moral dogmas on an unwilling, pluralistic society. That wasn't how it was, and I wanted all these leaders of their faithful, to demonstrate publicly, that our case rested upon principles that were fundamental to everyone – the integrity of the Family and the protection of their children – that such principles *pre-dated* all religion, having been with man since his very beginnings on earth.

After some crucial adjustments, asked for by different religious leaders, it was despatched to as many of them as I was able, in the short time left to me, before the Appeal case came to court, mid-November. This is what it declared:

A Public Statement by Religious and Community Leaders

'According to Article 16 of the Universal Declaration of Human Rights, "The family is the natural and fundamental group unit of society and is entitled to protection by Society and the state."

Equally the Commandment of God to "Honour Thy Father and Thy Mother" operates for the well-being of the child and society generally. This Commandment is frustrated and held in contempt when parental rights and duties are deliberately suppressed by having recourse to "secrecy". Moreover it is particularly in relation to sexuality that children need guidance from those who place them highest in affection; because loving a child involves protection from harm.

It is incompatible with the nature of parenthood and childhood that medical and other bodies should be permitted to modify healthy bodily functions, with the potential for causing grave harm, whilst parents are deliberately kept in ignorance of their children's activities.

The Hippocratic tradition of *PRIMUM NON NOCERE* – firstly, to do no harm – places a responsibility on a doctor to enlist the help and co-operation of a child's parents, particularly when the physical and moral welfare of the child is in jeopardy.

In this respect, girls need special protection, as the future mothers in society, and must be given opportunities and facilities by law and by other means to enable them to develop physically, mentally, morally, spiritually and socially in a healthy and normal manner.

We believe that it is a matter of elementary justice that children, during their formative years, should enjoy parental love and guidance. A child must be allowed to live its life and childhood free from harm, whilst parents must be encouraged to help their children reach a state of maturity which excludes harmful influences.

Where special circumstances exist and where a doctor does not fully know the girl's background, he should be required to obtain independent outside information from his "primary health care" team, prior to withdrawal for consultation with the parents. In those rare cases where parents are found to be uncaring, irresponsible or grossly disturbed, local authorities are already charged with full powers to act *in loco parentis*, where a child is exposed to grave moral danger.

We therefore pray that on these fundamental principles justice will be done, for the present and future well-being of all in society.'

The signatories to it included the Rt. Rev. Dr Robert Runcie, Sir Immanuel Jakobovits, Cardinal Basil Hume, Dr Syed Pasha, General Wahrlstrom, Rt. Rev. Hugh Montefiore, the Leaders of the West Indians, Afro-Asian-Caribbeans, Evangelical Alliances, Strict Baptists and Presbyterians.

When all were safely gathered in, I wondered what exactly I should do with such a precious document — this Statement of Faith? Why not send it to the Queen? She was a mother herself, and the Sovereign of her people; so who better?

Away it went, post haste; and before very long a charming reply was forthcoming, from Her Majesty's Private Secretary, Sir William Hestletine:

Buckingham Palace   3rd December 1984

Dear Mrs Gillick,
I am commanded by The Queen to acknowledge your letter of 30th November and to thank you for sending for The Queen to see the copies of the statement signed by a number of Religious and Community Leaders concerning the debate over the right of parents to be informed before contraceptives are prescribed by doctors for girls under 16. Her Majesty has read this statement with interest, and, in accordance with The Queen's instructions, the Statement has been forwarded to the Secretary of State for Social Services.

Her Majesty much appreciated your kind good wishes for herself and her family for Christmas and these_The Queen warmly reciprocates.

Yours sincerely,
W. Hestletine

Now we all know how difficult it is to get a letter to a Government Minister, with all those busy little secretaries of his in between. Better to use your MP for such a task. Better still, to have the Queen herself send it.

Though we shall never know just what Mr Norman Fowler replied to Her Majesty we can be fairly certain it wasn't just a DHSS postcard saying:

'Thank you for your letter, which is receiving attention . . . .'

November saw another quite extraordinary declaration.

170

This time it came from 2,000 doctors, and was aimed at their own General Medical Council.

For over a year, doctors had been subject to the Council's new disciplinary code of conduct, on the giving of advice and treatment to under-age girls, on contraception and abortion. Doctors had to remain clandestine about both procedures, or face the disciplinary consequences.

A Suffolk man had written to me about these new rules in March of that year:

> 'I wonder though, are doctors *really* forbidden by the GMC in the interests of confidentiality to disclose what's happening to a girl in a case like this? Whether her partner in crime is of her own tender years, or adult, perhaps someone old enough to be her grandfather? If this is true it would appear to be quite dreadful, especially if the same Council tells doctors it is "their duty" to break confidentiality under other circumstances.'

Well it *was* true, and a large number of doctors were not only irked by it, they were positively adamant that such rules had to go! Now it is extremely difficult to get even a handful of such independent souls to put their names to any controversial statement. Thus, for two thousand of them to lobby their auspicious Council in this way was quite unprecedented.

The writing was clearly on the wall for the GMC:

> 'Your guidelines have been carefully weighed up in the surgery, and found to be wanting in liberality!'

It was not until the February of 1985, after the Appeal Court judgement, that the Council finally agreed to amend their Rules; and decided that medical discretion was a better alternative to medical coercion; and thus allowed a small proviso to be included, to the effect that, if a doctor could not agree to treat a child in this way, and still remain silent before the parents, he now had a second option – to pass her on to another doctor who *would* comply with her demands. But he still had to keep his decision secret from the parents.

This didn't help parents at all; but at least it allowed the doctor with a conscience to wash his hands of the problem, albeit in private.

Whilst all these petitions and declarations were taking place, the date of the Appeal loomed ever nearer. It was to be heard on the 19th November at the Royal Courts of Justice in London.

Letters from the public began to pour into our house again. From Buckingham a father wrote:

'Very many thanks indeed for continuing to front the fight against medical interference with basic parental rights, in the context of under-age contraception. I believe all responsible parents will join me in wishing you all success in the Court of Appeal.

I am saddened at the way in which moral standards have been debased, frequently with official connivance, and a reversal of this trend will be widely applauded.

Thank you for your tenacity.'

Three letters contained those thoughts and experiences which have become so well known to all of us. The first was from a Wiltshire mother:

'I also have two daughters, one is a very attractive 15 year old, the other also an attractive 11 year old. I read the Report in the *Daily Express*, and I agree completely with what it said. I think you are dong a wonderful job. Sex could be best left until older, about 20, when children have matured mentally and physically.

No one has the right to decide against a parent's wishes; surely we are supposed to be responsible for everything else. This I think is the most important point, especially where disease, cervical cancer, VD, and many other things are involved. Today for the majority of boys, sex is all they want, it goes on in schools, children talk about it and boast who they have had sex with.

It's about time parents were given *back their* Rights.

We have to keep them, feed them, clothe them etc. That's hard enough in the Society with hardly any jobs, the last thing we want is sex. Our very good luck.'

The second letter was a personal experience from a Leicestershire mother:

'I have 2 daughters, one aged 18 and one 19. they attended Catholic schools and were taught at school, contraceptive methods, abortion etc.

Last year the elder daughter questioned me about the Pill – she did not want to go on it without my knowledge. I must also tell you that neither they nor their two elder brothers now attend Mass on Sundays, nor have they done so for some time now. The real dilemma for young girls today is that it has already been accepted by all of their age, that the Pill is the answer to having sex without risk of pregnancy. I believe *she* told me because of *needing help* in her decision to have or not to have the Pill. She needed help and came to me for advice. She has many boyfriends and many would-be boyfriends, but is certainly not promiscuous at all. She, and many more I think, are in the invidious position of trying to justify *no sex* to boyfriends when the Pill is so freely available. In the past, though girls suffered the consequences, it was acknowledged by many, that the boy was to blame. Now it can be said that the girl did not take precautions. Girls today are probably more sexually harassed because they can take the Pill. If girls can get it without parents' consent, how can they be protected from boys, whose only aim in life, is to boast of the number of conquests made? Not all girls can talk on this subject with parents – certainly those who would wish to keep their taking of the Pill secret. I hope you can put forward better than I, the argument that girls are already subject to more sexual pressures today, than ever before, because of the availability of the Pill. It has not made them free to choose. It has done just the opposite! Do we really want 12–16 year old girls to suffer so?'

173

How could I put it better? This liberal folly of giving sexual instruction, even in Catholic schools, devoid of any philosophical debate on the nature of human beings and the age-old wisdoms that taught that sexuality should only be between husband and wife in a loving and stable relationship; that only taught primitive taboos, rather than a positive message that chastity and fidelity were the way to true health and lasting happiness. Instead, the older generation of our *own* parents let slip the jewels that they themselves possessed, and under a welter of permissive propaganda, fell for the idea that, at last, human nature had changed completely, and from now on, true freedom was to be found in total licence on all fronts. Nor does it come as any great comfort, that these liberated libertines, are now to be seen holding up their hands in consternation, as they see their *own* fruits ripening, and find that the young nowadays, find deep pleasure in expressing that freedom in terrorism, juvenile debauchery, pornography and rape.

What I want to know, and so do a lot of other people, is where were our Religious Shepherds, and what were they doing, and saying, to counter the Sixties propaganda, when we all most needed them? I don't remember hearing a single word, spoken from the pulpit, that gave me, as a teenager, any guidance or practical help, that I so often sought. Speaking up against it now, twenty five years too late, looks to me like the Shepherds lamely staggering after an already scattered and ravaged flock.

A Catholic priest from Cheshire wrote of his own involvement with young people, and what he saw as a factor in the *current* breakdown of family life:

'From 1971 to 1976 my full-time work as a priest was the setting up and day to day running of a hostel for 14-18 year olds in Glasgow. But you were also very relevant to my present work of setting up a parish in a New-Town setting. Many of the deprived youngsters in my life do live in their own 'New-Town' houses, rented or mortgaged with 2 TVs, micro-computers etc., etc. – all helping to tranquillise the deprivation. The need is great, but the "Gillicks" responding to it

174

are few, so the Brooks, FPAs and Woolfs are often left to answer "the need".'

Throughout all this time, I had used every channel available to me to urge people to *pray* for the case, through religious newspapers, national prayer groups and personal correspondence. I asked them to unite in this universal cause. Such a wave of spiritual energy, unifying and strengthening each of us, could not be denied at the gates of Heaven!

From Wiltshire again a mother wrote:

'I feel that God is at work in society and if parents don't have full responsibility for their children, we can only leave it to God to find a way, and He will.

I keep writing letters to various people, trying to influence them, and I'm sure there must be others doing the same thing. *Good* must prevail for the preservation of the family. Sex is for marriage, for the protection of children, but it is a very unpopular thing to say.'

Another mother from Sussex wrote:

'I thank you so very much for all you are doing for the sake of our children. Your courage and perseverance are an inspiration to all mothers; I only wish I had written to you long ago as I had intended. There are many young mothers who, like myself, do not get around to writing, but support you in spirit and prayer. Thank you again.'

The feeling of a great movement of minds and hearts was almost palpable. Not the way those poor bemused folk, in some newspapers, believed it was: a kind of well organised and super-financed, American style 'Moral Majority'. Just the ordinary everyday wishes, hopes and prayers of the common people, united in spirit, for a just cause.

From Buckinghamshire came two heartfelt pleas:

'As a mother of three children, I want to thank you for fighting for our natural parental rights. Our thoughts and prayers are with you and will be especially when you go to the High Court. We pray that you will win.'

'Could I convey to you, both as a Christian and a midwife, that I stand with your high principle of motherhood, and want to assure you of my prayers at this time.

You are not alone in your concern for truthful relationships between parents and children/young people, alongside the National Health Service and doctors throughout the country. Many of us within the Service are also fighting for the same thing.

May the Lord hear our prayers for you, and our mutual Christian principles, which we hold up for this country.'

It is very likely that I was not alone in having my doubts about the success of this Appeal. I knew in myself, that what parents wanted was no more than common justice. But would the Judges see it that way?

From Surrey came an equally sceptical thought:

'I am a lawyer and I am filled with admiration for the magnificent battle you have waged in the High Court. As we await the Court of Appeal judgement I fear the worst, for I know how powerful are the forces which oppose you – not least in the medical profession. Whatever happens there are millions of people on your side.

I believe that the spirits of Florence Nightingale and Josephine Butler inspire you. Not for nothing were you christened Victoria!'

How could he have guessed that dear Josephine was, indeed, in my every prayer! Those waiting days were awful, alternately full of hope and then foreboding. On occasions, simple mental and physical exhaustion seemed to rob me of strength. That was when family and friends were really appreciated. Throughout the whole, long campaign, they had stood 'in the wings', the unsung, unheard heroes and heroines. My children had taken a lot of abuse, from some of the more cruel members of the community. By and large it was a kind of jealousy against them, because of the media publicity. I suppose if I had been a motorcycle champion, or popstar, *some* young people would have felt it equally necessary to yell abuse, in order to be noticed. But my lovely children took it all like little stoics, and grew more philosophical by the day. They experienced some of the worst, but also the *best* that is in human nature; and the best was infinitely more apparent to them, throughout those long weeks and months of waiting.

A dear priest from the North, whose spiritual guidance had been a continual source of strength to our family, wrote just before the Appeal of his own spiritual 'Renaissance' some years ago, in the face of his own apparent failure:

'For a long time, something has been niggling at me about your Appeal. I hope it's the Holy Spirit. All my life I've been an expert in failure. All *my* enterprises have crashed about my ears and plunged me into the depths, until one Good Friday in St Austins, Liverpool. Everything was collapsing – youth club, school, parish, and I felt right down. In this depression, I found myself kneeling at the altar rails. I looked up and there was the empty tabernacle. I thought:

"You BF. Who do you think you're following anyway? The greatest failure of all time. No human failure could be greater than for a cause to collapse with the terrible crucifixion of its leader." Immediately an enormous peace enveloped me and all St Paul's words, about weakness giving *His* power its opportunity, came over me. And a great joy. Since then, He's been teaching me repeatedly, stubborn mule that I am, that He's the boss – that He does not necessarily want my plans.

I am sharing this experience with you, in case your Appeal is rejected. What I want to say is this, so that you react with your customary resilience. The cards may already be fixed against you. *But* even so, Jesus has already *WON* and does not depend on human laws or judgements to win His war through you. He, in you, has already won, even if you don't live to see it. If you know this, we can all silently ask the Father in the name of Jesus and in the Immaculate Heart, for the Triumph of the Holy Cross at your Appeal. Please God He will rout the enemy then, for all to see, but if not, we must rejoice just the same. It will mean that He has a much better trick up His sleeve to be revealed at the hour God has determined. Then you will all be happy whatever the result.'

I must say that whenever I sent up a prayer to God, it wasn't simply for the 'case' as though it was some disembodied thing, devoid of human participation and judgement. Like the lady who wrote to me from Essex, just four days before it began, my prayers were directed at very human targets indeed:

'This is just to assure you that we are with you heart and soul and pray that the Barristers and Judges will find both courage and wisdom on 19th November, and you yourself strength of heart and a quiet mind now, on this long-awaited day.'

Nine: 'The Appeal'

'Nothing so wears me out, body and soul, as anger, fruitless anger; and this thing fills me with such an anger, and even hatred, that I fear to face it. The thought of this atrocity kills charity and hinders my prayers. But there is surely a way of being angry without sin. I pray thee, O God, to give me a deep, well-governed, and lifelong hatred of all such injustice, tyranny and cruelty; and at the same time give me that divine compassion which is willing to live and suffer long for love of souls, or to fling itself into the breach and die at once.'
Josephine Butler 1869

Without doubt the Victorian social reformers faced far greater physical brutality than reformers do today. Josephine herself was frequently cornered by gangs of men, and threatened with injuries to herself and her women supporters. The Salvationist, Bramwell Booth was hospitalised several times, while he campaigned against the 'White Slave Trade' of child prostitution.

When I had read all about the sufferings of these brave folk, it made the attacks on our own family seem mild by comparison! Nevertheless it isn't much fun having one's front door continually kicked, one's husband and children spat upon, fist fights in the street; public demonstrations organised by abortion fanatics against 'Victoria's values', with badges sporting such jolly gems as 'I'm glad Gillick isn't my mother!'; women journalists accusing me of every social sin imaginable, such as having too many children, and living in a cosy little backwater etc., etc. Cosy little backwater! Does any such thing still exist?

Now, I know it was a fairly brutal time, in the cities, fifty years ago. I know that the last World War did a lot of damage to the moral certainties of many people. But how do we explain the explosion of violence and promiscuity amongst schoolchildren, in the aftermath of the enlightened Sixties?

Or is it really true, that the future of mankind is both with – and within – *womankind*? If men devalue and debauch them, sterilise or abort them, will men become more kind, considerate and civilised? As they witness their mothers, sisters, wives or daughters falling foul of the fashions of the age, or participate in the downfall of others, will they be more likely to run to their defence – or stand jeering on the sidelines?

For all the social planning, for all the brand-new housing estates, the technological miracles and the pre-determined births, are we a more personally responsible people, with cleaner cities, happy homes, intelligent newspapers, friendly policemen, gifted teachers, honest workers, charming children and faithful parents? Are we, in fact the supreme epitome of civilisation at its most noble and fulfilled? Or are we what some people predicted we might become: bereft of a truly human moral conscience and abandoned to mere animal instincts?

A Catholic friar wrote to me from Glasgow around about this time, with encouragement, as the brick-bats flew:

'It is of course all your effort and, as history teaches, it is individuals such as you that begin ''movements'' which challenge (and hopefully replace) the ruling thought patterns and values of the age. I am proud of you and as a fellow Christian, Catholic and young(ish) priest want to thank you. Perhaps this is better coming from you rather than clergy, no matter how high their rank. Unless it comes from the lay folk, people will think it is just the Catholic hierarchy trying to impose their outmoded beliefs on the population.

One really is able to see the powers of darkness at work behind the ''new ethic''. It is terrified of people like you because you expose them for what they are. As our Lord says in John they prefer the darkness to the light. Just how you took on the establishment I do not know; I think I would have a nervous breakdown!

180

Listening to the BMA guy on the news this evening – one would think that doctors have some absolute right. Teachers can be forbidden to cane kids (correctly in my opinion) but doctors can lay kids open to promiscuity and lies. From my experience in a parish on the South Coast – doctors have not the slightest interest in persuading the girl to tell the parent.

I have seen so much suffering caused by mothers putting their girl on the Pill at 14 as soon as they have a boyfriend. They have given up any hope of chastity. Somewhere it has to stop and at least be pushed back. Remember John Paul at Wembley when he said in the homily – 'Can we just shrug our shoulders and do nothing . . . . ?' I pray too and our community prayed tonight for your good health and that of your family. Your enemies will be watching you like hawks for you to put a foot wrong. I pray that you can endure. May our Blessed Lady who knew so much distortion and detraction and hate against Jesus watch over you and protect you.'

Was the elderly gentleman from Huntingdon remembering the past through rosy spectacles, or is there some truth in his memories?:

'As one who was born and bred in the Edwardian era (but now alas widowed and bedridden) I know at first hand how high our moral standards were in England, and I am appalled that they have now sunk, not merely to the gutter but to well below sea level.'

The day of the Appeal arrived at last, and Gordon and I travelled by train to London. Once again, he could only stay with me for the first day, before hurrying back home to look after the family.

We squeezed ourselves into the packed court room, beside the law students, friends and foes, pressmen and passers-by. This time, we were in a modern court, with swinging high-backed red vinyl chairs for the Judges, and stack-away ones for the Press, and eye-aching strip lighting over all.

181

Nerves were taut and faces strained as we got under way, before Judges Fox, Eveleigh and Parker.

Our barristers had determined to stress the point that parents had a 'duty' to protect their children. They had duties and obligations. After a few minutes Judge Eveleigh interjected:

> 'What about parents' *rights*?' Were we afraid of the word *rights*? Parents couldn't perform duties unless they had the means to do so, he said, and that meant they had to have "rights" surely? "Yes, M'lud," we conceded, almost apologetically.'

From then on, for four days solid with questions and answers, legal history both ancient and modern, speculations, ponderings, examples and hypotheses; from ten thirty in the morning until four thirty each afternoon, the arguments flowed back and forth. Every legal point was stretched to its logical conclusion, to see how it would end up in practice. If *we* said that a doctor was aiding and abetting a crime by giving an under-age girl contraceptives, then so was a parent, who gave consent to it. If *they* said a child could give consent to contraception and abortion, then presumably they could give consent to all other medication as well?

And so it went on, though not without its funny moments, when occasionally a Judge made some humourous or witty observation, and beamed as the whole court room chuckled out loud. In one such instance, Counsel for the DHSS was striving to argue around the thorny question of 'wardship'. One of the judges asked whether, if a 15 year old Ward of Court could go to a doctor and ask for contraception, could that doctor prescribe without leave of the court?

'No,' said Counsel John Laws. 'Why not?' asked the Judge. 'What's the difference between the Court's decision and that of the natural parent?' 'The Courts always get it right,' replied Laws. 'Then if you lose this case I hope you don't seek to go to the House of Lords . . . .' came the dry, judicial response. Prophetic words indeed.

By the end of the fourth day, only a handful of stalwarts

remained in the Court Room. Even the Press, worn dizzy with legal wranglings by the DHSS, had been reduced to a mere three or four. I myself was so weary with concentration, and four sleepless nights, that I almost dozed in my seat.

Then came our barrister's summing up.

The final question put to him by the Senior Judge has stayed with me to this day. 'So you are asking us to protect the family?'

'Yes, M'Lud,' came the grateful response.

The Court was then dismissed and judgement deferred, indefinitely or for at least a month, we thought.

Back home, alone, to Wisbech, and all the gloom and foreboding was lifted for a while. There were so many letters to answer from well wishers. The Public Statement had yet to be sent to the Queen. Radio and television programmes; controversy raging in the press; the Agony Aunts going berserk once again – only this time in a letter to *The Times*. I replied to it, and it was published. 'Ardent if ageing, Lily the Pinks', I called them. Not very charitable I suppose; but I was angry at their hypocritical 'compassion' they so kindly measured out to girls in their newspaper columns whilst the clinics did so in little sachets of pills. Compassion – my foot! Their rusty needle had simply got stuck in the grooves of an old, old record – as old as sin itself. If *they* couldn't see that, there were *Times* readers who certainly could. From Warwick came one rebuff to them:

'Your recent reply to the latter-day "Lily the Pinks" which appeared in *The Times* was truly an inspired piece of work. That will surely make them sit up and think! Imagine them all ganging up like that and setting themselves up as the caring compassionate ones? Perhaps the old crones are worried your fight will end up with them all being out of their nice little numbers, well-paid into the bargain. I mean, imagine if they had *no* letters from highly impressionable young children to answer? Then they might just have to work like everybody else!'

Another from Bradford wrote:

'Please maintain your teasing and sardonic attacks on that preposterous coven of "agony aunts" who have taken to banding together as if they were especially influential or important, or, even, had quasi-official status. They aren't – and they haven't! Don't let them forget it.'

We were kept waiting three weeks before the court reconvened on the 20th December. It was to be the last day of such sittings, before the Judges ran off on their Christmas hols – and left the rest of us to gather our scattered wits together.

Down we flew to London once again, in something of a flap, as we had not now expected the judgement to be made until *after* Christmas. The judgement came in thick bundles, as each judge had had his say, and totalled 70 pages in all. Copies were handed around to barristers and waiting pressmen. Nervous fingers flicked through them to the back pages and then – We'd won . . . We'd *won*!

Amazement and stunned disbelief all round. All *three* judges had come to the same conclusion, which was summed up by Lord Parker:

' . . . as a matter of law a girl under 16 can give no valid consent to anything in the areas under consideration, which apart from consent would constitute an assault whether civil or criminal, and can impose no valid prohibition on a doctor against seeking parental consent.' Further that:

' . . . any doctor who advises a girl under 16 as to contraceptive steps to be taken or affords contraceptive or abortion treatment to such a girl, without the knowledge and consent of the parent, save in emergencies, which would render consent in any event unnecessary, infringes the legal rights of the parent or guardian. Save in an emergency his proper course is to seek parental consent or apply to the Court.'

Thus the DHSS Memorandum of Guidance 1980 was 'contrary to Law'. Judge Parker also expressed his gratitude to both counsels for their assistance, and for 'eschewing the sort of arguments which will doubtless follow the judgements given today'. Shrewd man! Those 'sort of arguments' had already begun several weeks beforehand, with predictions of untold havoc, should the Appeal favour the parents' position.

Now, all hell would break loose. And it did . . . .

Meanwhile we arrived home, exhausted, late that evening to find journalists on the doorstep, and TV men in local hotels. The sitting room was festooned with decorations and a Christmas tree twinkled in the centre. A long paper banner had been made by the children and stretched across the mantelpiece – 'Well Done! Well Won!'

The following few days were just unspeakably confusing, with television cameras and reporters jostling for elbow room and cups of coffee, while children tripped over wires, dodged the legs and scrambled over the furniture.

At last, Christmas Eve arrived and we were left in peace, perfect peace, to enjoy what was left of Christmas – the best part – with all praise to the Christ Child and His comfort in all things.

Then the reaction began. A 'phone call from a journalist on the *Mail on Sunday*, asking to come and see us to talk about the case. I agreed. It was Boxing Day, and I said I would see her the following afternoon. Catherine Bennett and a photographer duly arrived, complete with notepad – and tape recorder.

Impatiently, the children, my husband and I were 'organised' on to the sofa for a family photo. We were still full of Christmas high spirits, which made the photographer more impatient still. Sticky fingers and funny faces by an irrepressible crowd of ten children, was obviously *not* his cup of tea. There was an unexpected air of suppressed hostility in the pair of them.

The interview began and a few questions were asked about the case. All of a sudden, Miss Bennett began asking me about my *mother-in-law*! At first I couldn't grasp what she was saying. Then it all became clear. It was to be a 'hatchet job'. They wanted to find something nasty in

185

the family cupboard, and had visited my husband's poor mother, on Boxing Day, and bullied their way into her flat, taken photos of her, and generally intimidated her with questions about her religion, how often she saw her grandchildren, whether she agreed with her daughter-in-law and so on. They left her, frightened and worried – off to do the same thing to me, the following day. I was stunned, incredulous that such journalists could be employed by *The Mail*.

When the article appeared the following Sunday, it was just what we expected. Poor Grannie was made out to be a lonely old lady, abandoned by her son and his wife to celebrate Christmas alone in her flat, while we sipped port in our 'mansion', and boasted of being a 'good family'.

The result of this piece of 'compassion' was to leave one old lady weeping for several days, after she had just spent a very jolly Christmas with her other son and his family. There never had been any family divisions, as the article tried to make out; and mercifully, this appalling affair only served to make the bonds of our family the stronger, in adversity.

But we were still hurt by it, like Grannie herself, and felt quite numb and helpless. Some blows are so far below the belt, that all action seems pointless and impossible. Then I recalled the words of the Glasgow friar ' . . . your enemies will be watching you like hawks for you to put a foot wrong.' I hoped we could endure . . . .

It wasn't all horrid though! There were hundreds of letters that came pouring in from far and wide; the Christmas cards, 'phone calls, and happiness and relief that was so obvious, from so many, many people. From a Surrey vicar and his wife came the following:

'Just to say Hurray, Hurray – and well done for all your hard work. What a relief. We are so thrilled that all the Judges came out in your favour and our view is vindicated at last. This really has made a turning point in our history, and I am so hopeful that we are now on the way back to a more moral society, that encourages stable family life, rather than trying to undermine it.'

A Kent vicar gave voice to his concern on the pastoral care of parents:

'As I have written in my letter to the press, too many doctors look upon this as purely a clinical matter, and they treat us as machines, without any controlling spiritual or moral considerations.

I write as a parent and a parish priest, now "retired"! It never seems to be realised that everybody born into this country is born into a parish, with a parish priest, or his equivalent, in easy access. I know full well there are many different types of priests, and some are not easily accessible on such matters as advice on "sex". But the parish priest really worth his salt shares the life of his parishoners and is concerned with the *whole* of life and all its problems. And there is a spiritual and moral factor in all problems which the medical profession too frequently disregards, and our legal system too, though it must be right in the assertion that consultations with under 16s was "contrary to law".'

A Catholic priest from Manchester sent his message to the family from all his parishoners:

'In this parish we had a Holy Hour with Exposition of the Blessed Sacrament on the Saturday before you went to the Appeal. We have continued to do so each Saturday with the intention for parents – that they will recognise the privilege God has given them, as co-creators with Him, and that the state support them in this. You must have felt very lonely during your years of campaigning. Be assured that, even though the leaders are hesitant in their full public support – the foot-troops and the vast majority of our people, do give unqualified support.'

From a Leicestershire Pentecostal church, the pastor wrote:

'We do rejoice with you and congratulate you on the victory you have accomplished, by the grace of God. It is good to see right triumph over that which is wrong. If we can help you in any way please let us know. Our prayers are with you.

The Lord bless you in your endeavours.'

Another priest wrote, this time from Humberside:

'The medical profession in our post-Christian age has almost totally abdicated any responsibility for the whole good of the person – partly because they, the GPs, are often far too busy and hurried; partly because they are dealing with the young from broken homes already, and partly from their own lack of ethical seriousness.

The Lords may support you, they may not, but the torch is lit and the light shines – may you be blessed.'

A similar concern about medics came from a Hampshire man:

'I need not tell you that the battle is not yet won. The forces of evil will be gathering up their specious arguments and propaganda, paying no regard to the moral aspect of this problem.

One of the things that has sickened me over all the correspondence etc., over your case, is that everyone has assumed that it is proper for children to engage in sexual activities. No one has ever seemed to draw attention to the 6th Commandant. They suggest that pregnancies can only be avoided by the Pill, not by moral imperatives. We are supposed to be a Christian country, but licence seems to be the rule.

I find that doctors' principles are very suspect, and they are not guided by principles at all. The fact is that unless all good men and true are prepared to stand up, like you, to the evil forces in the world, then the flood-gates to everything will be opened – euthanasia, abortion, foetuses in deep freezers, children as pawns to everyone's whims and lusts.'

It is a crying shame indeed, that the BMA and all their camp followers have left so many people with the absolute conviction that almost all doctors are now suspect and not to be trusted with our children. What a terrible disservice they have rendered their profession, by opposing parents so often and so vigourously; and have very definitely lowered their reputation and their ethical standards, in the public's eyes.

So let it be said, loud and clear, not *ALL* doctors are like that. Some doctors *do* care. Lots of them in fact. Here are four, for starters!

From a Hampshire GP:

'May I offer you heartiest congratulations and thanks for your efforts in the Law Courts. You have given the Nation a victory for responsible parenthood over sick permissiveness. Well done; a wonderful success which will endure even if DHSS appeal is heard.'

A Cumbrian gynaecologist:

'I would just like to encourage you in the fight that you are having with the DHSS. I was pleased to see the Court of Appeal had ruled in your favour. I was amazed at the hysterical outburst from the BMA in response.

If they take it to the Lords – I would just like you to know that we would be praying that, there too, commonsense will prevail.

The Lord bless you – take courage and do not be afraid, for the Lord our God is mighty and He is able to do far more on our behalf than we can ever imagine is possible.'

Two London GPs also wrote:

'I was absolutely delighted to learn of the success of your appeal. As you have said yourself, it is the finest possible Christmas present, particularly for you, but also for all your well wishers. It represents an outstanding tribute to our legal system that in a plural society, if someone who holds tenaciously to her views, is prepared to fight, then justice prevails.

Naturally the battle is not yet over, but one can foresee a greater rallying to your banner.'

The other:

'I have considerable experience of prescribing the Pill. I am very glad you have given society this timely reminder that children are a God-given responsibility which cannot be delegated to, or usurped by, the State.

What is so encouraging about this case, to me, is that you are an individual mother acting out of concern for her children, which I think makes the outcome that much more meaningful to people.

We shall be praying for you; I trust that Mr Clark and the DHSS will not give you too much trouble – ''Righteousness exalts a nation, but is a reproach to my people.'' Don't forget there are few GPs who actually condone under-age sex, and 2,000 signed a petition supporting you, so don't let anyone try and fool you that ''doctors don't agree with you'', because they're wrong.'

The unfortunate position taken up by the hierarchy of the Mothers' Union caused many a heartache and headache to its grass-root membership, who were usually in favour of supporting the family and responsible parenthood, just as was their foundress, over a hundred years ago.

One member did all she could to change the views of those 'at the top':

'Many, many congratulations – well done indeed! I have been behind you every inch of the way as has my daughter, herself bringing up three girls.

My background is – ex-Headmistress of a Girls' Public School, a long working life spent with girls. Mother of two daughters and regular churchgoer (C of E). From the very first I wondered how I could best help your campaign and then (needless to say) I was shown what I ought to do, and challenged the Mothers' Union, who – quite incredibly – *supported* the Resolution that doctors should be allowed to prescribe

190

contraceptives to children under 16 behind their parents' backs. Every single ordinary member of the MU I have been able to contact has backed me up.

I have encountered either weak apathy ("they must know best") or an irritatingly patronising response, from those in positions of authority, and this very day I received a letter from the Central President, reiterating all the old arguments we have heard over and over again already, evading every direct question I had asked and concluding "I hope I have been able to reassure you that the Mothers' Union has not abandoned its standards or its witness for the Church." *What* witness? I am not in the least reassured, but your wonderful victory today makes the MU's pontifications irrelevant, thank God.'

It is certainly very sad about the Mothers' Union. I can only think that, having seen rather a lot of the squalor and moral mess of cities such as London, where the MU has its headquarters, they have decided that anybody who isn't entirely middleclass, responsible, reasonable, upright and English is just a hopeless case. The prophetic spirit of their forebears, and their sense of mission in the world, seems to have vanished, and been replaced with a fashionable liberalism, dressed up to look like Christian care.

But not to worry. Most of us have become quite accustomed to being totally unrepresented at top level, in many organisations – not least in local councils, authorities and government!

Most of the letters I received after Christmas, were from mothers and fathers. Some were just very simple cards, unaddressed like this one:

'Just another Mum with three young daughters who is delighted that you have won your Appeal, and grateful for your determination.'

Or the one from the Merseyside mother of six:

'Congratulations and very best wishes – you fought

the good fight and won in the end. I know many parents' hearts are lighter today because of your effort and spirit. God bless you and your family.'

Another unaddressed card:

'I salute you and thank you. Because of *your* success in the Appeal Court yesterday I feel much more hopeful for the future of my 14 year old son and 10 year old daughter. I also wish to thank your husband and children who, I'm sure, have been a great help to you, with their support in this long battle.'

Again from Merseyside:

'I am not a Roman Catholic, not even very religious, but I do have a 14 and a half year old daughter and have supported your efforts all along. Congratulations. My husband and I are one of the millions of families who are grateful to you. God forbid if our parental responsibilites are taken from us.'

From others came a cry for honesty in relationships, like this one from Surrey:

'I have four daughters, two of them only 12 and 13 and a half years old, and I am also a Catholic.

Doctors who give contraceptives to underage girls are encouraging unscrupulous men to exploit them, when they are most vulnerable. They are also breaking the law. Taking the Pill is a public declaration that the girl is ready, willing and able to be promiscuous.

These men don't love these girls. Love is patient, love doesn't grab and destroy, love protects and respects the loved one. Contraception is not an alternative, the only safe alternative is that little word '*NO*'; these girls don't need birth control, they need self-control and self-respect.'

A long and thoughtful letter came from a gentleman in Essex, concerned about authority in the home and society:

'I have two sons and two daughters, now all in their 30s. They and my wife support your view that girls under 16 are particularly vulnerable. They *require* parental and social support, at that age, against strong pressures from the boys. The encouragement of unrestrained sexual experience for the young, is only one aspect of the profoundly mistaken attitudes to authority, parental and social, which have been so sedulously propounded by popularity-seekers. The young human, left to develop without any restraints, becomes neurotic – always seeking some limit to activity. When none is provided, the youth is like as not going to throw a brick through a window to see what happens – and may thus encounter for the very first time, in the shape of a policeman, the social constraint which has so far been lacking.

In fact, authority, or discipline if you like, far from being repressive, as those stupid liberal humbugs suppose, is in fact creative. Self-discipline has to be taught, but once learned, it is the key to creative living. As to authority itself, I believe that a distinction should be made between authority which is arbitrary, save in its exercise, and against which there is no appeal – on the one hand; and on the other, authority which is constitutional, and limited to what responsibility requires.

Parental authority, whilst not strictly "constitutional", nevertheless is not and has no right to be arbitrary. But it must match the responsibility of the parents – and that they never should be allowed to evade. As to spiritual authority – without it there is no hope!'

A Cambridgeshire mother explained one of the anomalies in the business of 'medical consent':

'One of my daughters (aged 15) is at present filling in an application form to come to the Isle of Ely College in 1985. It is ironical to note that on the medical form supplied with it, I am required to state any drugs or medicines she is taking prescribed by a doctor, because she is under 18. In the case of a girl receiving the contraceptive pill within this age group without the parents' knowledge or consent, how on earth could they complete and sign such a form correctly! It doesn't make sense.'

Before the judges had come to their almost universally unexpected decision, the Minister of Health, Mr Kenneth Clark, and his officials repeatedly stated in private and in public that his Department would 'Review the Guidelines' depending on what the judgement said.

Yet within 48 hours of the verdict going unanimously against the DHSS, he had made a monumental U-turn and announced his intention of challenging that decision in the House of Lords. What perfidy! What duplicity!

A Suffolk mother put it kindly, thus:

'As the mother of teenagers I would like to congratulate you on the result of the Court hearing. I have been behind you all the way, feeling sure that parents should have full responsibility for their children's welfare. I do not like the attitude of the BMA or the Family Planning Association and think their arguments are nonsense.

As a supporter of the Conservative Party, I am surprised at their proposed plans to appeal against the result and hope that, on reflection, they will support the decision. I am quite sure the Prime Minister would support your views.'

Some hope! Surely to goodness it must be obvious to everyone by now that if a Conservative government such as this, is prepared to fly in the face of the majority of its loyal supporters, and risk political suicide by so blatantly breaking one of its basic manifesto pledges, of upholding 'traditional values' and support for the family, then it is because there is within its permanent officialdom, a core of very hard line social engineers, with a policy on population control that extends way beyond any party political considerations. Thus it is that every DHSS Minister, whatever colour his party bosses may sport, always ends up by promoting birth control facilities for the working classes and the poor. Even if that means taking everyone's legal rights away, in the process; and even if it means joining forces with lunatic elements on the extreme Left to achieve that aim.

Another Suffolk mother – this time a Labour Party supporter – also saw the idiocy of so many conflicting policies:

> 'How odd that "children" are now their parents' legal responsibility, up to 18 years, when it comes to a decision not to pay them dolé money, unless they register for a YTS course. Yet in certain circumstances they are suddenly adult and independent at about 12!! What logic!!!'

On the very last day of 1984, a remarkable letter reached me from Winson Green Prison in Birmingham. Even there, feelings run high on this crucial issue. This man, converted to Christianity during his term of imprisonment, took time to warn me of what surely lay ahead:

> 'I am so happy for you and all Christians everywhere, that you have been victorious in your "Good Fight" – at least for now!!
>
> Satan has a lot more up his sleeve with which he is going to attack you, and do not be surprised if your victory is only temporary, for what is happening today is written!!!
>
> Whilst my own mind goes far beyond the present (yours likewise?), I am so happy that there is someone like you to fight for the lambs those idiots are trying to lead to the slaughter. Mr Clarke and the rest of those *morons* better understand this – *he* was one of the *loudest voices* condemning *PIE* and its *evil* members. Yet he, as an MP cannot see the horrible path he treads by offering the Pill to those under sixteen, with or without parents' consent!!
>
> He is trying very hard. Now he is going to the House of Lords? Timothy 4:3, 4.
>
> If they succeed Victoria, then it is out of your hands.

Jesus will look after you and your family. We are not far off the 'dog's vomit' of a society we deserve, and anyone who does not see where it is all leading to, does not deserve to be in a position of power! They expect fresh and salt water to come from the same spring? They soweth the wind and they will reap the whirlwind!!!! Who am I? I am a man who, like Saul, fought against Our Saviour, and (yes, in here!!!) was chosen!!! About three and a half months' ago. Grace and peace to you from God the Father and Our Lord Jesus Christ.'

A retired Anglican minister in Devon gave similar predictions of abuse:

'There's no need to acknowledge this letter, as you must receive many. If I know anything about them, they will include abusive and bigoted ones from the so-called progressives and subversive types, who undermine religion and morals. Be sure, you have much support though.'

Nor did we have to wait very long, before some truly hideous letters arrived. They were usually anonymous and nearly always contained some reference or other to my having a large family. The text of most of them was unprintably obscene. Written in fierce and uncontrollable rage, without introductions, except for such delightful epithets as 'Dear Breeding Machine' or the even lovelier one of 'You self-righteous bloody slut'. They were so awful, they often made us laugh in crazy disbelief. The following one, so incongruous in its ending, was just such a case:

'Dear Doe,
Here's hoping at least one of your litter will eventually give you cause to regret your unthinking uncaring Catholic views.

Your self-righteous smirk needs wiping off your face. You should have thoughts for the under-privileged.

From a caring and thoughtful
Mother'

196

A daily cartoon strip, in that bastion of liberal thought and female emancipation – *The Guardian* – ran for a week depicting myself *and* my children as rabbits. Presumably the author of it, Steve Bell, would have found himself happily at home with some of the dirty and ugly prejudice I occasionally encountered in my own mail bag, which described me or my husband variously as 'acting like a rabbit' or 'calving down'.

Behind the veneer of such 'respectable' journalism, with its bitchy, tittering, office boy humour, lie thoughts not a million miles away from those so graphically expressed by the anonymous person who described us as a 'dirty pair of over-sexed bastards', or the one who suggested 'Why not have your old man castrated?'

For some inexplicable reason, known only to these New Puritans of the Revolution, indulging in lots and lots of contraceptive sex is OK – but having lots of children is dirty and uncontrolled. Strange, how liberalism didn't manage to include *tolerance* in its manifesto . . . . or did it? One poor, distracted writer from Liverpool, who simply signed herself 'A rape victim', scrawled out her maddened message to me – 'Ten children in 15 years is a good reason for compulsory birth control.' The New Puritan ethic on birth control, came over in its characteristically confused form, in this letter from a mother from Milton Keynes:

'You have *TEN* daughters and *YOU'RE* obviously enjoying love making so, why should you try to deny it to a girl of sixteen?! . . . . Ten daughters and *ALL THAT* sex *IN* between!! . . . . I have three daughters, 16, 17 and 19 years of age and I can assure you they are *STILL* virgins!! I have *NO* need to complain!' etc., etc., etc.

Some people were really nasty, such as the nameless London vet who wrote on a postcard:

'We need another Herod to sort you lot out.'

A bright spark even put my name down in a prostitutes' contact magazine, which resulted in a truly obscene letter, plus a £5 note from a sick, sad fellow in Dublin! Another young man, from a nearby town, photographed his unspectacular naked body and sent it to a false address in the South of England, where the Post Office opened it, read my address on the contact magazine ticket, and posted it on to me! I passed it on to the Police.

A very common theme amongst the couple of dozen such letters I received was *MONEY*:

'Why should the average citizen have to pay your taxes and family allowances because of your lack of control of your sexual urges?'

A Surrey man began cogently enough, but then went off the rails a little:

'I don't like promiscuity in society, particularly when it comes to schoolchildren etc., but after all we are all *human*. After all, who are you to dictate how people shall behave when you have *TEN KIDS*.

How bloody thoughtless, stupid, selfish and utterly *NAÏVE*. What a fine example you represent to world population, stability, salvation and human suffering perhaps later. Jobwise, do you expect *all* your kids to find jobs in the future? What right have you got to claim child benefit from the tax payer? You should be *TAXED* for having too many kids. It's a bloody disgrace to mankind that you should be allowed.

I suppose it's bloody stupid outdated Catholicism that puts you up to it. The sooner they blow up the Vatican and sack the silly Pope the better. You believe in God that way. Once alive then meet thy maker mentality.

80% of people *don't* believe in old fashioned nonsense, it's only for the *WEAK* and *IGNORANT*. Religion has caused more pain and misery than all the wars, famines put together. You are not responsible enough to judge other people's morals.

Disgusted'

Poor, abused Ethiopia cropped up in the following diatribe:

'Madam,
To see your wild eyed ravings on TV the other night made one realise what a fanatical crank you are.

No doubt the fact you have brought forth 10 children explains it – you probably have nymphomaniacal tendencies and enjoy making the beast with two backs with your husband so much that you have a guilt complex about it.

What an example to your own daughters! I would hope a friendly doctor or other reasonable adult will give them tuition in birth control, otherwise the country will end up knee deep in religious nutters like you.

God will in any event cull any population explosion. He is doing fine in Ethiopia and elsewhere except for your type which is trying to subvert His will.'

Again – poor Ethiopia:

'I write concerning your recent court action over the birth control pill and would say that I am a 44 year old married man.

No matter what any of us do, young people will continue to have sexual intercourse, under age or not. Fortunately, in the past, many youngsters had the commonsense to seek contraception to avoid the danger of unwanted pregnancies and the misery and heartbreak that this inevitably brings with it. You, by your selfish actions, are now committing many young people to this misery and heartbreak with, in most cases, ruined lives. The birth rate in the world is reaching the stage where the world can no longer support the large numbers of people being born into it and this, to a large extent, is the reason for the disaster in Ethiopia. You, by your actions, are helping to worsen this situation in our country and, I note, you have not set a very good example yourself by bearing 10 children.

You are a very stupid and selfish woman and I am
surprised that a court of sensible people should take any
notice of an idiot like you. You should be thoroughly
ashamed of yourself.'

What was it the Ghost said to Scrooge?

'O God, that the insect on the leaf should speak about
the too much life amongst his hungry brothers in the
dust.'

Some people, usually men, seemed to *want* the young to
suffer, just in order to satisfy their own personal hatred of
me. From London one such wrote:

What an appalling thing you have done. You have
the true face of evilness, without compassion or
understanding.
May ever pregnant girl under 16 be on your
conscience. And may every young girl's death from
suicide or back street abortion be counted amongst
your sins.'

One doctor from a private abortion agency, and herself a
magistrate, wrote to *The Guardian* complaining about my
use of Legal Aid in the case, as though this was in itself a
crime against true justice.

Her agitation tied in well with the taxes and child
benefit objectors. Yet for the life of me, I cannot
understand their arguments. For a start, Legal Aid is
granted to around 90% of all law suits and criminal cases;
including divorces, child murderers, wife beaters, sadists,
football terrorists, street muggers, drunken drivers etc.,
etc. So why shouldn't a mother who wants to be
responsible for her own daughters' welfare receive a little
bit of assistance, as well?

Then again, all hospital treatment for illnesses incurred
through personal neglect or over indulgence, are paid for
by all of us together; including injuries sustained through
fighting, drunkeness, drugtaking, over-eating, under-
eating, smoking etc., etc.

Contraception is only free, like abortion, because we *all*

have to pay for them. Likewise treatment for venereal disease and cervical cancer. We *all* have to pay for the indulgences of others, in this 'pluralist' society. Thus, other people's morals – or lack of them – are imposed upon the pockets of the masses. With my large family, and no state benefits, saving Family Allowance (which even the wealthy receive) and a semi-derelict house in need of rebuilding, together with rates, gas, electricity, telephone bills etc., not to mention a hundred and one items, all with indirect tax on them – I think we pay our way. Like most other people, we also complain that too much of it goes to Government!

Thankfully the cranky hate mail, and the nasty ones, were not many.

Most people were like the mother who wrote to me from Norfolk:

> 'I just want to say that I wholeheartedly support your campaign and I sincerely hope that the Court's decision will not be overruled by any appeal. I was absolutely delighted at your recent success in the Courts and felt at last that some sanity was returning to the country – just a small glimmer of hope that the trend towards lower and lower moral standards is starting to be reversed. It is wonderful that you are prepared to spend so much time and energy to fight for a better world for our children, because it seems to me that so few people are prepared to stick their necks out and say what they really think in public, although privately they are very worried about what is going on. It is very unfashionable nowadays to talk about morals and to say that young people should be restricted in any way by the law or by their parents – there are so many people who will say you are cranky, narrow-minded and 'behind the times' or just simply being a kill-joy, when of course nothing could be further from the truth. I take my hat off to you, Mrs Gillick, and would like you to know that I am with you all the way.'

The kind people who wrote such letters will never know just how much such encouragement meant to our family.

Ten: 'The Aftermath'

> 'To surround anything, however monstrous or ridiculous
> with an air of mystery, is to invest it with a secret charm
> and power of attraction which to the crowd is irresistible
> False priests, false prophets, false doctors, false
> patriots, false prodigies of every kind, veiling their
> proceedings in mystery, have always addressed them-
> selves at an immense advantage to the popular
> credulity, and have been, perhaps more indebted to
> that resource in gaining and keeping for a time the
> upper hand of truth and commonsense.'
> *Barnaby Rudge* by Charles Dickens

How often have I bemoaned the fact that I was never
given enough 'air space' to discuss the full implications of
my campaign and the three court cases which have
punctuated it, over the last two years. Instead, I have
been faced with the questions the *interviewer* decided to
ask, and they were always of the same standardised kind.
Never a chance to broaden the issue out, or look at
alternative procedures. Instead, I was confronted with the
'hard case', the most imaginatively horrendous situation
that any child could find herself in, and then *I* was
supposed to sort it out in terms of law and medical
practice.

The media has played a large part here, in narrowing
down the arguments to such an extent that we find we
have only two alternatives: to prescribe or not to
prescribe. But then, as I have said before, the media is
really only concerned with 'good stories', and in their terms
that usually means a conflict of one sort or another –
the 'them and us' syndrome: dividing labour from
management, police from public, religion against
religion, race against race, generation against generation.

Now we have children versus parents, and parents versus the medical profession.

Like an exciting sport, the media sets individuals or groups against one another, giving 'opposing' sides equal air time. 'What is your next move?' is the frequent question set them, with the hope that they can keep the story going nicely for the newspaper or media programme. So we are reduced to two 'teams', ever on the go, scoring points, and in the end coming out winners or losers.

In a sense, this whole book has been an exercise in showing that life simply isn't as black and white as that. Families, parents, children, doctors, teachers; they are never either just 'good or bad'. They are people, who fail and who succeed, every hour of every day, throughout their lives.

A court case, such as ours, was not concerned with the practical differences between family and family, child and child, or doctor and doctor, even. It was dealing, as all such cases must, with a *principle*. Law must be based upon principles, and not merely utilitarian practices or fashion. If such were not the case, then for sure we would have been living under a tyranny long, long ago – foolish and incompetent, maybe, but a tyranny nonetheless.

But those who opposed us, every inch of the way, disregarding principles, ethics or morality en route, have been those whose practice has been based almost solely upon practicalities and personal interest. I include the DHSS, the BMA and the world of birth controllers amongst such groups.

My case would seem to be a simple one, asking no more than most parents would consider obvious. That no doctor should give contraceptive and abortion advice or treatment to any of my five daughters, whilst they were under 16, without my first being consulted, and never against my wishes, unless a court of law ruled otherwise.

Those who disagreed with this simple wish evaded answering it, but relied instead upon spreading the most extreme of horror stories, hoping thereby to frighten the public into silence and final acquiescence. Their tactics were dishonourable and dishonest, even if entirely predictable.

Even before the legal dust of the Appeal case had had a chance to settle, the voices of panic were beginning to be heard. Many tactics were tried, in an effort to bully the public out of its commonsense. First amongst them was personal vilification in the press, by women journalists. They jeered, ridiculed, and scorned. Nobody in their right mind would have anything to do with such a monstrous anachronism, they seemed to say. A Victorian throwback, with outlandish views on morality and family life. A person, callous and indifferent to the harm she had caused. 'O God, will this woman never learn!' screamed one of their headlines.

I began to feel rather like the Jackdaw of Rheims, who stole the bishop's ring and was thoroughly cursed for his crime. Was there any part of me they didn't loathe and despise? Like the proverbial fishwife, bawling smelly abuse at passersby, these frustrated and angry women journalists continued unchecked. One sympathetic editorial in an East Anglian newspaper described the situation:

'Mrs Gillick is now quite clearly the principal beast-figure in the demonology of termagant feminists and their fellow spirits.'

Oddly enough, one of these termagants was known to fellow male journalists as 'Vampira'!

Whether or not these women succeeded in raising the status of female writers and broadcasters or convinced the public that they were creatures of intelligence, wit, or compassion, is hard to say. Certainly, any number of readers thought they were pretty awful. A mother from Cambridge wrote:

'A few months ago I happened to tune into a TV programme in which you featured, together with Anna Raeburn. You were subjected to some very offensive scorn and having principles was held to ridicule. The attitudes and remarks made me furious.

I too hold to all the "old fashioned" virtues of honour, integrity, loyalty etc., but when I have had occasion to stand and defend an injustice, it has been depressing to observe how alone one is. In fact the usual reaction is that one has adopted the mantle of the village halfwit or is the bearer of some deadly infectious disease. I expect this has also happened to be your experience, but I suspect that, like me, it only strengthens your determination and resolve to stick to what you, and the majority of caring parents, know is right. So many parents these days abrogate their responsibilities towards their offspring and find it easier to surrender providing guidelines to their progeny to someone – *ANYONE*!

Thank you for taking up the cudgels on this issue. You have epitomised "to thine own self to be true."

A vicar from Blackpool and a priest from London felt equally sure, that the corruption of the young, by the loony left-overs of a foolhardy generation, was something beyond mere human folly. The vicar wrote:

'Please do not despair. It is a fact of life today that anyone who stands up for sound moral and spiritual values will be attacked by people who are clearly under the influence of evil.

You speak for large numbers of people who share your views and admire your courage. They, like you, have noticed the disintegration of our society and can see that the tide cannot be turned unless home and family are restored to their rightful place.'

And the priest:

'It is an awful manifestation of the power of the Evil One to see how so many leading medical and political people are clamouring to let mere children ruin body and soul – they know very well the physical dangers, even if they can't see the deeper harm of souls. Why do they do this? "Sexual experience" a new idea coined to confuse!'

Why do they do this? For a whole variety of reasons, I suspect. Ignorance, anger, intolerance, expedience, indifference. Every reason can be found – and used – by those who wish to pursue a government policy, which they believe absolutely to be the only solution to a social problem.

Most young people don't think twice about *why* they do this or that thing. They simply react to the social climate in which they find themselves. But who creates that climate, who sustains it, and who profits by it – now *these* are the questions that interest me. Doctors, on the other hand, are not immune to the fevers around them. They are as variable as their patients – some responsible, some not, some moral, some indifferent. Their job – an unpleasant and disturbing one in so many ways – is to pick up the pieces of other people's broken health – broken, so often, by their own folly or excesses. The blame for all our ills can no more be laid at *their* door, than at those of the poor, the ignorant or the wayward generally.

It is the social manipulators that have done the work: the liberal philosophers in society; the media propagandists who sowed the novel ideas to a harmless, but ill-defended generation if the Fifties. So, what began in sexual licence and student disturbances in the Sixties, unchallenged by the Churches or Universities, gradually and inevitably seeped downwards through the age range, sibling to sibling. Now we have the Sixties phenomenon, acted out in the secondary school and below, with promiscuity and violence a common and growing menace.

The DHSS saw what was happening in the early Seventies, and thought it could control the situation by providing birth control to 16 year old school *leavers*. Ten years later, it is having to provide it to twelve year old school *starters*. One magazine recently suggested that the ornaments of sex be taught to four year olds . . . lunacy indeed!

Of course, the 'feminist' movement had a lot to do with it. They created the jargon, the slogans: 'A woman's right to choose' and 'Not the Church and not the State – women shall decide their fate'. They were calling for abortion to be licenced. Now they are calling for a girl's (oops! 'under-age woman's') right to that awful operation. Sex was once thought to be the burden a woman had to suffer in silence. Now pregnancy is the great fear. Where once rape, in Great Britain, was a rarity with only 9 reported cases in 1964, now there are hundreds and hundreds of cases each year; in fact 30 a day, in London alone. Pornography abounds; and still they call for more sexual liberation. So silly . . . .

It is *so* silly, indeed that nobody is entirely hoodwinked by it, any more. For far too long we have been bamboozled into accepting any old rubbish as a philosophy, and have sat back in frightened or respectful silence to the greatest idiocies pouring out of the highest places. Now the chickens have come home to roost, as they say, and we can all see quite clearly what bedraggled and wretched creatures they are. Satirists are at a loss to know what to make fun of, since everything they once lampooned is actually happening, and it isn't even funny any more. Where twenty years ago such media anarchists as David Frost once sported with the Establishment, he has now become a part of it. His generation (that is, mine) now sit in television studios, sentimentally mooning over the 'good old days', and lamenting over the bad ones here and now!

So much has changed over the past two years, that, where once many people were too frightened to say what they thought, now more and more of them are happily prepared to challenge every decision made about their lives, by others. The wind of change is certainly blowing. You can sense it all around, even when things seem to be at their gloomiest and most impossible.

It is often said that 'things have to get worse, before they get better'. It's true, but only so far as the people *themselves* make them better. My own feeling is that is precisely what people are striving to do. The *striving* is the most important thing. Apathy is the greatest breach in their defence.

No matter how loudly the 'opposition' rage, no matter how desperately they have to work, to muster their dwindling supporters, their time is fast running out. They are seen clearly for what they are: the pained and hopeless remnants of an irresolute and wayward age. Let them gather together for warmth, under whatever political banner gives them most comfort and bravado; the mood of the nation is such, that it will let them pass away, unmoved from its own present resolve, to do things differently – this time round.

As soon as the Appeal was over speculation once again abounded about the likely date of the DHSS challenge in the House of Lords. Just as in 1984, the British Medical Association's bigwigs thought it would be at once. Then Easter was given as a possible date, finally Midsummer's Day itself, the 24th of June.

Whilst the hopes of some were high that an early hearing would immediately reverse the judgement, an odd assortment of individuals and groups mustered together under the 'anti-Gillick' banner. One of the first of these appeared in print in February's *Marxism Today*. The former Press Officer for the Family Planning Association, Rose Shapiro, letting off steam at the inadequancy of the 'moral left' to counter the rising influence of the 'moral right'. The liberal establishment knew it was falling in popularity with the public, she stated. But what to do about this calamity? So she rounded on her friends, the BMA, the FPA, the 'Brooks', and berated them for being so limp-wristed, and for daring to suggest that underprivileged girls might be suffering as a result of promiscuity rife amongst them. These groups were capitulating to fear, she wrote. 'This is the stuff of pragmatic semi-liberalism and not sexual revolution,' scoffed Ms Shapiro.

Her scornful tongue-lashing, of the Lazy Left, seemed to have the desired effect. In next to no time the 'Brooks' was at her side. At a public meeting in Islington, organised by the local Communist Party, Caroline Woodroffe (Gen. Sec.) was to be seen sandwiched together with Ms Shapiro and Ms Woodcraft, under the Marxist banner. From their platform they harangued the audience on the 'bigoted and sexist' Gillick Ruling.

And what did the Great British Public make of it all? I'm afraid we shall never know, since only seventeen of them turned out to listen and one of them rudely fell asleep in his chair, half way through . . . .

As I said once before, I have great faith in the British; they are an eminently sensible people, on the whole.

Next it was the turn of the BMA itself to leap onto the careering 'Gillick-bashing' bandwagon. A *semi*-private committee meeting of doctors on community health and medicine, met on the 11th January, to swop horror stories about the consequences of the Appeal case. So many incest and suicides anecdotes flew around the room, that afterwards nobody could quite remember who had said what, to whom. But *somebody* knew. And somebody told somebody else . . . .

When, *almost three weeks later*, the newspapers carried a story of a 14 year old girl who had apparently committed suicide on the 30th January (the inquest in April gave an 'open verdict'), a journalist on the medical magazine *Pulse* was told by *somebody* that this case had been discussed at the BMA meeting! It was said, although wrongly, the girl had died because she could not get contraception, for fear her mother would be told of her father's incest with her. *Pulse* published the story, speculating at the same time, that the 'case' might well influence the thinking of the General Medical Council, the following week in February, when they sat to decide, on their revision of their draconian rules to doctors.

The Press Association – a central news gathering agency – then picked up the story from *Pulse* and phoned the BMA Press Office for confirmation – that the suicide of this girl (on the 30th January – three weeks *after* the BMA meeting!) had been *discussed* at that meeting. The BMA confirmed it had. And then went on to tell of another suicide case, that had also been discussed at that notorious meeting – a 12 year old girl, whose parents had refused to give their consent to her obtaining contraceptives(!) had then killed herself. Both suicides were supposed to have taken place between the time of the Appeal judgement on the 20th December 1984 and the 11th January 1985 – in just twenty two days . . . .

Fleet Street, having been given the awful news, attempted to check the facts with the BMA Press Office, and received evasive confirmation, mingled with crocodile tears of sorrow and foreboding. So Fleet Street published the stories and overnight *I* became a 'murderess'.

How the women of Fleet Street loved it! A really juicy piece of journalism to deal with – incest, suicide, children, the Pill; nasty, evil, stupid Mrs Gillick etc., etc. . . . .

At Manchester University Debating Society, some weeks later, I attempted to speak, and was pelted with condoms and pills, from Socialist Workers Party fanatics, with cropped hair and wearing white T-shirts with obscene slogans painted on them. (I looked for their Nazi armbands, but they hadn't got round to that – yet.) They screamed and bawled for twenty minutes before the rest of the audience voted them out; the University bouncers obliged. All the time, Dr John Dawson of the BMA and Dr Fleur Fisher, a family planning doctor from Macclesfield (and one of *that* committee) sat impassively as the word 'murderess' howled about my ears . . . .

About a week later, I decided I had had enough of all these accusations in public, in private, through the press and media. The BMA refused to confirm the 'suicides' to me, refused to give me details of the time and place of the inquests, hid behind their sacred oath of confidentiality – for the sake of the girls' families, said Dr Havard, Secretary of the BMA. Letters from members of the public began coming in, accusing or commiserating. A 15 year old Cheshire schoolboy wrote, having 'discussed the matter' with his parents:

'Do you realise how many lives you are ruining? Two girls under the legal age of consent have committed suicide because of your actions. Does this help you to sleep at night? You are entitled to have your own opinions and bring up your children as you think best, but it is not your democratic right to enforce your ideals upon other people. You say that young women (for they are women) should talk over the matter of sex with their parents . . . . '

(Funny how 'two girls under the legal age of consent' suddenly turned into 'women', wasn't it?)

A pharmacist from Middlesex gave some useful advice:

'As a pharmacist, I don't think you know that the contraceptive pill can cause severe or even suicidal depression. Vitamin B6 in large doses can help this, better than anti-depressant drugs.

However, doctors don't warn about the depression, and prescribe "the pill" sometimes without a medical history or a *family* medical history. This kind of "depression" or neurasthesia is hereditary. How can a clinic know the family history like a GP?

When I read that a "pill" girl had committed suicide, I thought this was what had happened, i.e. the Pill had *caused* her depression by biochemical means.'

(But she was supposed to have died because she *couldn't* get the pill, kind lady!)

A Bedfordshire teacher also wrote with some thoughtful observations:

'I am only one of many thousands of mothers who are wholly on your side in your fight to restore some moral responsibility to parents of young girls.

The two examples of youngsters wishing to commit suicide – if these cases ever existed – only serve to highlight a lack of care or concern on the part of their doctors and families. Your care and concern has brought these issues out into the open, and rightly so.

In my work as a Head of Year and School Counsellor in a large school, I saw both the absolute neglect of the moral and psychological welfare of some of our pupils by their parents, and the angry frustration of the majority of parents who felt that they were losing control over their children through the careless attitudes of society around them. Mrs Gillick, you have had the courage to publicly strive to maintain this control; please do not let those who seek to escape their own responsibilities, by heaping their guilt upon you, deter you.'

A would-be mother from Surrey wrote about the Manchester debate, and her own conclusions on the Pill:

'I am sorry to read how bitterly you are persecuted. It is astonishing how malignant or apparently indifferent society can be once Christians start to stand up for themselves. We see it both in the extreme behaviour of your Nazi-style female thugs and in more "acceptable" attacks made by the media on church leaders who dare to take up their rightful rôle as prophets. It is terribly hurtful and painful, especially to children who are attacked on account of their parents' action. I suppose all we can do is remember that if the world hates us, it hated Jesus first.

I am in complete agreement with you regarding under-age contraception. I should even welcome a complete ban on the "pill". It is a highly dangerous and unpredictable drug, and no one in their right mind should even prescribe it, let alone take it. I stopped taking it last July and am still chemically sterile because of it. It never ceases to amaze me how the most vociferous champions of its universal use are those "wimmin" who are least likely ever to need it!!'

One newspaper in Birmingham even went so stupidly far as to publish a letter from a woman who suggested that doctors should send me black-edged cards because of these suicides.

Then a letter came from a Surrey gentleman:

'How disgusting that you have been subjected to such a vile campaign of abuse. Our prayers are with you.

About those supposed suicides quoted by the BMA. Surely there would have had to be inquests if the suicides had occurred? Call the bluff of the BMA. Ask when the inquests were, or will be held.'

I had been *trying* to find out about the inquests for some

time, via various MPs, who asked Parliamentary Questions, county by county. All to no avail. They were told that such enquiries would cost more than the £200, allotted to back bench questions! When even Clement Freud was unable to find out the details of such suicides for Cambridgeshire (on the grounds of costs, once again), I decided that I had waited long enough.

So I obtained a list of all the Coroners in England and Wales, from the reference library, and sat down one Friday morning and began telephoning each and every one of them. Four days later and the job was done. The cost was around £100. There were *no such suicides* (except the poor girl who apparently hanged herself on the 30th January where there was *no* connection with contraception at all, according to the Coroner's Clerk).

Most newspapers carried the results of my 'suicide search', and there the matter ended for them. But the BMA still refused to give up the stories, or apologise for them or admit their Press Officers were in any way to blame, for having talked to the Press about what was said at a private meeting. They call it 'professional secrecy' I believe . . . . More like the art of professional duplicity!

When I wrote earlier of the way the media and others seem to stereotype both individuals and their arguments, replacing original thought with cliché, I had in mind also, the way some impressionable members of the public pick up these phrases and clipped ideas, and repeat them without thinking further. I had received examples of this many times over, during the past six months, when schoolchildren wrote to me asking whether I would come and give a talk on my case to their class, or if I would send them detailed information for their examination work.

I declined to do either; firstly, because I do not wish to be a part of that sexually fanatical crowd, who regularly use schools and their captive audiences to preach their own particular philosophy and propaganda to schoolchildren. Parents should talk to their children about the intimacies of life – not strangers.

Secondly, I simply don't have time to sit down and write long tracts on sex for children, even had I thought it right to do so, which I didn't.

Here are two examples of what I call classically standardised thoughts. The first from a 15 year old London girl:

'I am writing to you concerning your successful campaign to ban the Pill for girls under sixteen. Your views would help me greatly in my school project in my exam work, taking in the problems of society of under-age sex and the outcome.

What were your reasons for taking your views so far? Do you think the law will not stop girls from having sex but instead they will use a less reliable form of contraception? Do you not think it is wrong that anyone of any age can buy a sheath? Would you campaign to change the law that says that boys can have sex from the age of fourteen?

I hope to hear a reply concerning your answers to the above.'

Ah me! The power of the media over immature minds. What *have* they been learning in their school sex lessons, that gives them such a diminished understanding or regard, for their own intelligence and their own bodies?

A London schoolboy wrote:

'I am writing to you on behalf of the Fortismere School Union of School Students; we are a student organisation and we are planning to hold discussions on current issues which concern school students.

Our first discussion is on the right of young women under the age of 16 to receive confidential advice and treatment on contraception and also about abortion.'

I ask you! 'Young women under 16'! I suppose I shall have to call 13 year old boys 'young men under 16' next! Perhaps if some English teachers spent a little more time teaching their pupils better use of the mother-tongue, and a little less time handing on media clichés or the techniques of contraception, we would not have to suffer the muddled thinking amongst the young.

And to think – these modern, 'know-it-all children, will one day be referred to as out-of-date parents, in *their* turn. The trouble with revolutions, sexual or otherwise, is that, whether we like it or not, they do have a tiresome habit of going round and round and round . . . .

A fifteen year old schoolgirl from Northampton could just as easily have submitted her letter to any number of TV documentaries:

'As I am only 15 years of age myself, I am well aware that some girls of my age do take part in sexual activities. Many of the girls I know would rather not have to go to their parents because they know that it would hurt their feelings, their parents may not feel the same about them.

If it was your daughter would you rather she was on the Pill or a chance of her becoming pregnant and have to tell? Do you not think it would hurt her to have to tell you?'

She was also doing a school project on the subject. How these children do fool themselves! They won't tell their parents because they are afraid they will say *no*, that's why.

I wrote back to her, and told her to ask her mother all the questions she had just asked me. I wonder if she ever did?

A Midlands mother wrote to me about some of the school literature she had found her daughter reading:

'When my daughter suffered from an eye complaint I was asked to read to her from her school book. I was, and still am, very upset at the sight of the garbage which teachers feel free to set before our children. I don't think headteachers receive many complaints because parents do not know what is going on. If they are aware, the task of altering the situation seems beyond them. Parents must be asked to *examine* their children's *printed* material for study.

If inspectors can find the time to eliminate perfectly harmless and indeed useful books from school libraries, they can surely address themselves to weeding out depressing literature bordering on pornography.'

215

One particularly irritating request came from a London man. His rude assumptions prompted me to tell him in no uncertain terms, what I thought of such slick, shallow, meaningless labels:

> 'I am a freelance journalist starting research which I hope will result in a book on "Britain's Moral Majority". As you are widely regarded as someone who holds opinions which could come under that heading, I should appreciate an opportunity to hear your views at first hand.'

The 'Moral Majority' is an Americanism. It doesn't belong here . . . except on our wretched telly screens.

The Moral Left – as they now like to be known by their friends – having been galvanised by their leaders into frenetic anti-parent activity, decided to band together in the same co-ordinated group as they had done before, when opposing all attempts to reform the abortion law. In this way they hoped to fool the public into believing that there was a massive grass roots groundswell of public opinion against the Appeal ruling.

A meeting was held by them early in the year, composed of committed spokesmen from the Community Health Councils, birth control agencies, abortion campaigners, socialists, trades unions and a couple or so Labour MPs. Members of their organisations and Health Authorities were leafleted throughout the country. 'Women in the Media' had an easy job, and most of the others fell into line soon after.

The National Abortion Campaign (a group which is reputed to want abortion on demand, up until birth) tried to organise schoolchildren in a massive Hyde Park 'anti-Gillick' demonstration, the day before the House of Lords case began mid-June. The National Union of Students and the Young Socialists worked with them. Posters, leaflets and briefings were fly posted all over London and elsewhere, with each one carrying its little horror story to frighten the immature and unwary into believing the sky was going to fall on their heads if parents ever had to be told of underaged girls' demands for pills.

216

Alas, the organisers forgot one vital procedure, when holding a demo. in a London park . . . you have to *book it* first. A 'Teddy Bears' Picnic' had got into Hyde Park before them, so another abortion group, who pride themselves on being rather more intelligent, was called in to take over. The 'Women's Reproductive Rights Campaign' then handled the street parade. As it turned out, only around fifteen hundred people could muster the energy to walk the London streets on that Sunday morning. So much for the 'massive opposition'!

Next it was the turn of the 'Brooks' abortion agency to release confidential information to the press. This time it was a *Daily Mail* reporter who was tipped the wink at their AGM in April.

A 15 year old girl had had an abortion and contra-ceptives *against* her mother's wishes, said the Brooks. The girl had gone to them, in private (though that didn't seem to matter, now that there was political capital to be made out of her), and asked for an abortion of her late pregnancy. When the mother heard of her request she refused to give her consent. So the Brooks sent the girl to a solicitor (or straight to the Social Services) and she was made a Ward of Court and the judge, Mr T.S.G. Baker QC, overruled the mother, and ordered an abortion and contraception – in the girl's best interest, naturally.

All this is gossip and hearsay of course, since the Brooks could only give titbits to the papers, but not the whole story, which was bound by secrecy, as wardship cases are meant to be. But enough was said in the press to make the mother pretty miserable, I don't doubt. Not to worry. It was all in the best interests of deprived girls from uncaring homes, wasn't it?

Whatever happens after the House of Lords appeal, there is obviously a crying and urgent need for a 'Family Legal Centre', to protect parents and their children from this kind of icy cold, calculated, manipulation and division of families, by abortion and birth control agencies, amongst others.

An intelligent letter came a while ago, from a mother in Cardiff. She took up the DHSS words of 'exceptional cases' and treated them with honest concern:

'As a parent, one wonders why they don't consider alternative solutions for the "exceptional cases", who now appear to be the only reason for the amended Section G. Such as (1) Individual re-education for the balanced and healthy way to emotional happiness; (2) Informing the boy/boys (and *their* parents too) man/men, of the legal aspects.

I am just letting you know about this, because if the "exceptional case" is as rare as they make them sound, there *could* be a more personal way of dealing with them.

I also wonder how the Health Department is *allowed* to use the words "Children . . . who will be exposed to serious health risks if no contraceptives are prescribed . . . .", when there appears to be abundant evidence of (more) serious health risks if contraceptives *ARE* prescribed.'

Ah, if only it were true that 'exceptional cases' were rare, but it is not true, and a girl only has to say 'I can't talk to my mum – she'd kill me', and she becomes *the* exceptional case. She is the model exception to a rule that doesn't exist. For the clinics, it seems to be 'Catch as Catch Can' and little more.

One mother from Norfolk had her solution to the problem already up her sleeve:

'Whoever is responsible for this sinful practice of advising children *not* to obey their parents in this vital matter, should take note of the recent report of harm being done to young girls, through taking this pill, and should any of my family be prescribed any harmful substances which could possibly damage their health, I will do my utmost to see that whoever is responsible will account for it.'

Fighting words!
The 'Children's Legal Centre' was another organisation, trying their hardest to influence the House of Lords case. Unmarried and childless representatives of theirs were always to be found in court, whenever our

218

case was being heard. They gave advice to children on how to get round the milestones of childhood – such as what they can and cannot do at certain ages. Smoking might be harmful to your health, but it's nice for your children to know when they can legally begin to harm themselves. They also seem to be rather aggressive towards authority generally; and I suppose we must be thankful to them, for turning our children into those nice, little, companionable people – the barrack room lawyer . . . . '

In April, the Children's Legal Centre petitioned the House of Lords to intervene in our case. They were calling for a child's right to give consent to *all* medication, irrespective of their age, their parents' wishes, or the medication on offer. Their petition was rejected; the reason being, I suppose, that the DHSS case was to be *exactly* the same! The issue has now broadened right out to its inevitably logical conclusion, as was seen in the December Appeal. You cannot have a girl, able to give consent on her own to long-term hormone therapy or an abortion on the operating table, if she then has to have her parents' consent to a Rubella vaccine at school, or a wart removed from her finger in a doctor's surgery. If she can give consent to the former, she can give consent to the lot! The DHSS is certainly taking great strides into the control of children – even if they have to achieve it behind the deceptive smoke screen of 'Children's Right to Choose'. Just how long that right to *choose* will be left in their own childish hands, is a matter for reasonable speculation. But I would bet not for long!

That is why I am always sceptical about those who concede anything to the State, in the matter of who chooses what is best for whom. Concede the principle, in favour of the difficult case, and you have conceded everything. There *are* ways to help the wayward, without necessarily allowing doctors, *on their own*, to make that final decision. However, a mother of three daughters must make her point:

'I am writing to you to let you know how much I uphold you in your stand to uphold parental rights in regard to the upbringing of their children. As a Christian I fully believe that the family was ordained by God and that children are given by Him to be brought up by the parents. At the same time, it would be foolish not to recognise that due to the evil that is in the world not all parents honour that responsibility and in those circumstances obviously provision must be made to ensure that children of such parents are properly protected, but such State intervention must be carefully monitored in order that responsible parents are not overruled in their authority and I am very grateful that you and others are publicly prepared to take such a stand.'

Unfortunately, the State has moved on − if it ever was stationery − from the idea of 'protecting' children in the way *that* kind mother suggested, to 'controlling' them.

Social workers, health visitors, district nurses and others, all know the confusion and inadequacy of the system under which they already work. With top-heavy bureaucracy and inadequate facilities, transmigration of people, and homeless individuals, the problems are legion. To believe that anything other than the easiest possible expedients will be used on problem girls is to hope for the moon.

Why else would a government, so cost-conscious as our present one, go to such lengths to establish *their* right to control these girls, via their medical staff? They have a plan, inhuman, uncivilised even. But they think it will work, if they can only get rid of all legal obstacles, such as the Gillick case poses.

Their plan won't work. The State cannot manage anything efficiently, not even the railways. So what hope have they, when dealing with adolescents and their families? I still believe that the right way to begin is to start by teaching the teachers how to give their pupils a sense of purpose, a sense of their own intrinsic value; to love and honour themselves, body and soul. Let them learn how to control themselves, and not be controlled by others, all their born days.

Most parents would welcome that approach, rather than any other. They do *not* like the way things seem to have been drifting over the past few years. A father from Suffolk was very sure of that fact:

'I have nothing but admiration for your continued stand against outside do-gooding interference in family matters. Doctors are people able to absorb information and take an oath. Those abilities do not equip them to take the place of a responsible *loving* parent. To assume that a doctor is more able to judge what is morally preferable for *my* child is arrogance. To assume that a doctor is able *with certainty* to judge what *in the long term* is physically preferable, is debatable at least.

I do not wish anyone to ''gang up'' with my child to deceive me. I happen to prefer my own values to other people's, be they doctors or not. I happen to love my children more than anyone else loves my children. I happen to think I have done a reasonable job in bringing up my children. I demand the right to carry out the above in my own way without outside interference. I have no social or medical qualifications, I have no deep religious convictions. I am, however, just an ordinary, caring, loving parent – what better qualification is there?

Ignore those who follow blindly their particular newspaper's views, ignore the eggheads with no hearts, the computers with no judgement. Society knows not *yet* the debt it owes to you.

Keep fighting, Mrs Gillick. *YOU ARE RIGHT.*'

At a meeting of Family Planning doctors in mid-April, a lawyer called Simon Lee spoke about the coming House of Lords case. He hoped I would lose it. He was a colleague of Professor Ian Kennedy, the well-known broadcaster and one time Reith Lecturer. Professor Kennedy is currently acting as Junior Counsel for the DHSS in my case. At that April meeting, Mr Lee made a surprising prediction. He said that if Lord Scarman and Lord Brandon were two of the five judges, then I would certainly lose my case.

It was without doubt a rash and unethical thing to say, to suggest that a judge's decisions could be predicted, before they had even heard the evidence. It was also a remarkable guess, for both of these Lords *were* hearing our case, mid-June.

For all the tub-thumping in vituperative newspaper articles, the street demonstrations, one-sided opinion polls, and all the weight of socialistic dogma and cant, for all the religious hatred, the lies, deceptions and dishonourable dealings that have taken place, over the past couple of years, in an effort to force parents into silent and glum acquiescence, yet we see more and more young girls – the future wives and mothers of society – put at risk, for the sake of a social decree. All these things have to match themselves against those who *will* not accept this bondage; but will strive, without doubt or fear, against a tyranny, a usurpation, an unnatural and unnecessary imposition upon the will of the people, which is to the detriment, pain and suffering of countless families everywhere.

Josephine Butler knew our struggle. She also knew the very source of her strength when she wrote, for us to read, a century after her own ultimate victory:

'There is no evil in the world so great that God cannot raise up to meet it a corresponding beauty and glory that will blaze it out of countenance.'

THE END

Appendix

A Letter of Protest from concerned women of the United Kingdom to the Prime Minister, TheRt Hon Mrs Margaret Thatcher MP:

'Dear Prime Minister,
In 1869, 120 women expressed their concern in a national newspaper (*Daily News* 31.12.1869) about the sexual exploitation of women. Their lobby paved the way for legislation which fully protected girls under the age of sixteen.

Today we, the undersigned, register our grave concern and protest against advice to health authorities published by the Department of Health and Social Security in 1974 and revised without significant change in 1980. These open-ended decrees require no account-ability from those to whom they are directed and permit the distribution of contraceptives to children of whatever age by doctors and professional workers without consultation with parents, if that is what the child wants. Are professionals now to be bound by the wishes of children?

We protest because:

1. A major change in public policy and legal safeguards has been imposed without due regard to public opinion, democratic procedures and proper parliamentary debate.

2. The personal security which the law on the age of consent seeks to give has been removed, leaving the responsibility ill-defined and putting the physical, psychological and moral welfare of children, in sexual matters, largely in their own hands.

3. Growing numbers of young girls are being enticed into early sexual activity by being offered the alleged protection of contraception without any real check on age, evidence of parental consent, or even knowledge. Many girls then find themselves trapped in the vicious cycle of: contraception – abortion – parental estrangement – promiscuity – exploitation.

4. DHSS policy contributes to young girls being exposed to exploitation by adults and by commercial and ideological interests. The crime of unlawful sexual intercourse with young girls is made more likely inasmuch as moral restraint is withdrawn the moment the state recognises and provides convenience for the practice.

5. Even the worst parents deserve to be given every chance by education and help to care fully for their child. In those exceptional circumstances where parents truly are uncaring or negligent, every local authority is charged with the legal duty to use all its resources to help and fully protect the children.

6. Sexual activity by and contraception for children is in the first instance a social not a medical problem. It is parents, and in extreme cases the local authority, *in loco parentis*, who must be given clear responsibility for a decision as to what is best for the child. A doctor will participate in the decision by offering guidance when it is sought but the decision should never be his alone, nor the sole prerogative of the child.

7. The provision of contraception to schoolchildren has failed: pregnancy and abortion rates have not dropped; VD remains a problem; cervical cancer is a growing trend; prostitution and violence continue. The social health of the country is no better. On the contrary, there is overwhelming evidence that the availability of contraceptives to children has been accompanied by an increase in these problems, with less and less recognition of the importance of parental influence.

8. There are no circumstances where contraception is a better alternative to full and proper care of the developing child. As in 1869, it is once again time for women and mothers to take the lead on this major issue which so profoundly affects the health, welfare and future prospects of happiness of their younger sisters and daughters. As Lord Devlin said in his letter to *The Times* (29.7.83), it is an issue which may well be socially the most important this decade.

Yours faithfully

Signed
Mrs General Maire Wahlström
World President, Salvation
Army Women's Organisations

Signed
Mrs Victoria Gillick
Wife and Mother

Signed
Mrs Valerie Riches, National Hon. Secretary
The Responsible Society, Family and Youth Concern